Christian

Foundations

By

Dr. Ronald L. Bernier

Published by **Vision Publishing**

Ramona, California

ISBN

978-1-61529-017-8

FOR INFORMATION ON ORDERING PLEASE CONTACT:

MASTER BUILDER MINISTRIES, INC.

397 Bay Street

Fall River, MA 02724

(508) 730-1735

www.mbministries.org

Or

Vision Publishing

1-800-9-VISION

www.visionpublishingservices.com

PRINTED IN THE UNITED STATES OF AMERICA

Contents

CHAPTER 1

THE IMPORTANCE OF A GOOD FOUNDATION

Throughout the Bible, God uses the building metaphor to convey principles of truth concerning basics and beginnings. Some of these Biblical examples are:

- *The foundations of the earth* (Job 38:4-6; Psalm 102:25; Proverbs 3:19; Isaiah 48:13; 51:13, 16; John 17:24).

- *The foundations of the righteous* (Proverbs 10:25; Psalm 11:3).

- *The foundations of God's testimonies or word* (Psalm 119:152).

- *The foundations of Zion* (Isaiah 14:32; 28:16; 58:12; Hebrews 11:10; Revelation 21:14, 19a).

- *The foundations of ministry* (Ephesians 2:20; 1 Corinthians 3:10-13; Romans 15:20; 2 Corinthians 10:16).

- *The foundations of the Christian life* (Matthew 7:24-27; Luke 14:27-30; Ephesians 3:16- 17; Colossians 2:6-7; 1 Timothy 6:17-19; Hebrews 6:1-2).

- *The foundations of the Christian community* (Matthew 16:18; 1 Corinthians 3:11; 1 Timothy 3:15; 1 Peter 2:4-7).

Literally, a good foundation is a secure base on which something is erected. It is obvious that a building is only as good as its foundation. The foundation in many ways determines the size, strength and character of the building that is set upon it. A weak foundation can only support a weak building. A strong foundation can support a strong building. A small foundation can only support a small building.

Bedrock provides the best foundation for any building. In order to build on rock, however, other less stable layers, such as gravel, sand, clay and porous rock, must first be cut away. In the Christian life, nothing of any substance can be built except what is built on the rock of Jesus Christ.

In many places in the New Testament, the growth of the Christian life is compared to the construction of a building:

> **1 Corinthians 3:9-10** (NKJV) [9] For we are God's fellow workers; you are God's field, *you are* God's building. [10] According to the grace of God which was given to me, as a wise master builder I have laid the foundation, and another builds on it. But let each one take heed how he builds on it.

> **Ephesians 2:22** (NKJV) [22] in whom you also are being built together for a dwelling place of God in the Spirit.

Many Christian lives over the centuries started out well in the beginning but were shipwrecked in the end. Perhaps you have known some Christians who were once walking with the Lord and seemed to be very strong in their faith, but now they seem to have lost their faith and are not walking with Jesus anymore. Perhaps you have even heard of some Christian leaders who have fallen in this way. What happened to them? Perhaps the problem was in the foundations of their lives.

THE CHRISTIAN'S FOUNDATION

What is God's appointed foundation for our Christian lives? Paul answers this clearly in 1 Corinthians 3:11:

> **1 Corinthians 3:11** (NKJV) [11] For no other foundation can anyone

lay than that which is laid, which is Jesus Christ.

The true foundation of the Christian life is the Lord Jesus Christ. Our foundation is not church attendance, dress codes, creeds nor doctrines. Our foundation is Jesus Christ, Himself, personally. Jesus is our foundation.

Your life in Christ is a spiritual structure in progress. In scripture, this structure is called "*a temple of the Holy Spirit*" (1 Cor. 6:19), "*God's temple*" (1 Cor. 3:16), and "*a spiritual house*" (1 Pet. 2:5). This spiritual building, like a physical building, will be only as strong, tall, and stable as its foundation. So build your foundation on Christ, the solid Rock, and you will be building for eternity.

THE NATURE OF THE CHRISTIAN LIFE

The best definition of the Christian life is found in John 17:3:

> **John 17:3** (NKJV) [3] And this is eternal life, that they may know You, the only true God, and Jesus Christ whom You have sent.

Eternal life, or the Christian life, is a personal relationship with the Lord Jesus Christ, and through Him, with the Father.

> **1 John 5:20** (NKJV) [20] And we know that the Son of God has come and has given us an understanding, that we may know Him who is true; and we are in Him who is true, in His Son Jesus Christ. This is the true God and eternal life.

Jesus came so that we could personally know God! This is also taught in the Old Testament prophecy of Jeremiah:

> **Jeremiah 31:33-34** (NKJV) [33] But this *is* the covenant that I will make with the house of Israel after those days, says the LORD: I will put My law in their minds, and write it on their hearts; and I

will be their God, and they shall be My people. [34] No more shall every man teach his neighbor, and every man his brother, saying, 'Know the LORD,' for they all shall know Me, from the least of them to the greatest of them, says the LORD. For I will forgive their iniquity, and their sin I will remember no more."

Everything in our lives should revolve around the Lord Jesus Christ.

- We should go to church to experience Him in greater measure.

- We should serve one another, because in doing that we are serving Him (Matt. 25:34-40).

- We should worship Jesus because that is our highest purpose as His people.

- We should live holy lives because that pleases Him.

- We should seek to lead others to Him so they too can know the joy and eternal blessing of a relationship with Jesus.

Everything in our lives should revolve around the Lord Jesus. He is our reason for living. He is our Savior, our Lord, our King and our God.

The reason many Christians have failed in their lives is because they did not build upon the right foundation. They tried to build their Christian lives upon church attendance, denominational allegiance, or a set of ethics or doctrines. But Jesus wants us to build our lives upon Him – upon a personal relationship with Him and to grow in our understanding of Him by studying His Word.

WHAT IS THE WORD OF GOD?

The most powerful force in the world is the Word of God. The Word of God possesses certain characteristics:

Isaiah 55:10-11 (NKJV) [10] "For as the rain comes down, and the snow from heaven, And do not return there, But water the earth, And make it bring forth and bud, That it may give seed to the sower And bread to the eater, [11] So shall My word be that goes forth from My mouth; It shall not return to Me void, But it shall accomplish what I please, And it shall prosper *in the thing* for which I sent it.

1. *God's Word cannot fail.* Just like the rain that falls to the earth, the Word of God is life-giving. Rain never fails to bring forth fruit and life. Similarly, the Word of God never fails to bring forth the life of God. God's Word is absolute. It never changes, and it is not relative. It means what it says and says what it means. It can be trusted and counted upon. It never fails.

2. *God's Word is full of life.* It cannot return void. Rain is the most essential commodity that heaven gives to the earth. There is no such thing as useless rain. It always accomplishes something beneficial. God's Word is like the rain. It cannot return void. The word void in the original language of the Bible means "empty-handed". This, God's Word, is not just empty promises. It always accomplishes its purpose. Just like rain infuses a wilted plant with life, the Word of God will infuse you with the life of God and refresh your spirit.

3. *God's Word will produce fruit in your life and fulfill God's purposes (Ps. 1:1-3).* Without water, no tree or plant can produce fruit. In the same way, the Word of God is necessary to bring forth fruit in your life. A fruit-producing life is one that brings honor to the Lord (John 15:16).

4. *God's Word has creative power (Ps. 33:6-9).* God created the heavens and the earth by His Word (Gen. 1; Heb. 11:3). When God spoke in creation, He created something out of nothing through the power of His Word. This creative work was

accomplished through the power of the Lord Jesus Christ (Heb. 1:2-3). As the creator, God not only created everything, but also continues to hold it together by the power of His Word. This is why you can believe God to continue to do new things today, even within the personal details of your daily life.

5. ***God's Word brings salvation in the new creation (John 1:1-14).*** Just as God brought all things into being through His Word, so He brings salvation to those who believe in Him through Jesus, who is the Word. Through Jesus, the Father has accomplished the great work of salvation. When you look at and listen to Jesus, you are seeing and hearing what the Father wants you to know regarding Him (John 14:9-11). The power of God's Word creates faith to trust Jesus. Without it, no one would ever turn to God (Rom. 10:17). God gives you a new heart and a new life through faith in Christ, which comes through His Word (Ps. 51:10).

6. ***God's Word penetrates your life (Heb. 4:12-13).*** The Word of God is the only agent in the whole creation that can penetrate the very heart of a person. Nothing else can divide a person's soul and spirit. Until the Word of God penetrates your life, you will continue to be controlled more by emotions rather than by the promises of God's Word.

7. ***God's Word points us to Jesus.*** The reason we study the Bible is so we can grow in our personal relationship with Jesus. The Word of God is given to man as a means to bring us to Jesus: to bring us to know Jesus; to bring us to experience Jesus; to bring us to a life of obedience to Jesus; to bring us to a fellowship of life with Jesus. Our knowledge of the Word of God should not be an end in itself. It should be a means to a greater end: the personal experience of Jesus.

As we study the Scriptures, let us always keep this in mind: everything we learn should bring us into a greater personal relationship with Jesus

Christt.

> **John 5:39-40** (NKJV) [39] You search the Scriptures, for in them you think you have eternal life; and these are they which testify of Me. [40] But you are not willing to come to Me that you may have life.

The Scriptures were given to us by God to bring us to the Lord Jesus that we might have life. But to know Jesus we must have a revelation of His Word.

THE NEED FOR REVELATION

> **Matthew 16:13-17** (NKJV) [13] When Jesus came into the region of Caesarea Philippi, He asked His disciples, saying, "Who do men say that I, the Son of Man, am?" [14] So they said, "Some *say* John the Baptist, some Elijah, and others Jeremiah or one of the prophets." [15] He said to them, "But who do you say that I am?" [16] Simon Peter answered and said, "You are the Christ, the Son of the living God." [17] Jesus answered and said to him, "Blessed are you, Simon Bar-Jonah, for flesh and blood has not revealed *this* to you, but My Father who is in heaven.

Many men and women saw Jesus as He walked the shores of Galilee, but only a few recognized Him for whom He was. It is the same today. Many people believe Jesus was a good man, or a great teacher, but that is not enough. Jesus is the Son of God. Jesus is God Himself.

We know that is true, but we did not come to that understanding through study or learning. We came to that understanding the same way Peter did: through revelation from God by the Holy Spirit.

This is how we will learn everything from God: through revelation by His

Holy Spirit.

Jesus sent His Spirit to teach us:

> **John 16:13** (NKJV) [13] However, when He, the Spirit of truth, has come, He will guide you into all truth; for He will not speak on His own *authority,* but whatever He hears He will speak; and He will tell you things to come.

We must have revelation because our natural minds are not capable of understanding the things of God:

> **1 Corinthians 2:14** (NKJV) [14] But the natural man does not receive the things of the Spirit of God, for they are foolishness to him; nor can he know *them,* because they are spiritually discerned.

That is why Jesus sent His Spirit to teach us His Word and His ways.

> **1 John 2:27** (NKJV) [27] But the anointing which you have received from Him abides in you, and you do not need that anyone teach you; but as the same anointing teaches you concerning all things, and is true, and is not a lie, and just as it has taught you, you will abide in Him.

We should not ignore the teachers God sends us to teach us His Word but through the Holy Spirit, we have a wonderful Teacher inside us who is well-able to show us everything God has for us in His Word. While someone is being faithful in preaching God's Word – the Holy Spirit is active giving revelation to that Word to us.

AFTER REVELATION COMES OBEDIENCE

It is not enough to receive revelation from God about His Word. We must obey it. Jesus taught:

> **Matthew 7:24-27** (NKJV) [24] "Therefore whoever hears these sayings of Mine, and does them, I will liken him to a wise man who built his house on the rock: [25] and the rain descended, the floods came, and the winds blew and beat on that house; and it did not fall, for it was founded on the rock. [26] "But everyone who hears these sayings of Mine, and does not do them, will be like a foolish man who built his house on the sand: [27] and the rain descended, the floods came, and the winds blew and beat on that house; and it fell. And great was its fall."

If we learn the Word of God, but do not put it into practice in our lives, Jesus said our lives will not stand the test of time, and inevitable winds of trial and adversity will destroy us. A life that has been built upon the solid rock of Jesus Christ is a life that obeys the Word of God. James wrote:

> **James 1:22** (NKJV) [22] But be doers of the word, and not hearers only, deceiving yourselves.

If you do not obey the Word of God, James says you deceive yourself. If you think you will be saved and grow in the Lord merely because you have heard the Word of God, you deceive yourself.   Hearing is not enough; you must also obey the Word.   Make a decision now that whenever God shows you something from His Word, you will obey it.

If you do not obey it, you will stop growing in the Lord, your relationship with Jesus will become damaged and your heart will grow harder to God. Eventually, if you do not change, you may end up forsaking God altogether.

Decide now to obey God. Whenever He shows you something from His Word, obey it. As you do that, you will be like the wise man who built his house on the rock, and his house was never moved no matter what came against it.

As we obey what God shows us, we grow in our relationship with Jesus, we please Him, and we bear fruit that will remain.

> **John 8:31-32** (NKJV) [31] Then Jesus said to those Jews who believed Him, "If you abide in My word, you are My disciples indeed. [32] And you shall know the truth, and the truth shall make you free."

Do you want to be free? Do you want to walk in power with God? Do you want to grow in your relationship with Jesus? Then make a decision now to always obey His Word.

CHAPTER 2

BUILDING ON THE FOUNDATION: THE WORD OF GOD

A personal relationship with Jesus Christ is the only true foundation for our Christian lives (1 Corinthians 3:11). But, once that foundation is laid, how do we build upon it? How do we grow in our relationship with Jesus and mature as Christians? The answer to this question is found in the word of Jesus, Himself:

> **Matthew 7:24** (NKJV) [24] "Therefore whoever hears these sayings of Mine, and does them, I will liken him to a wise man who built his house on the rock:

We build on the Rock of Jesus Christ in our lives by hearing and obeying His words. That is why we need to study the Word of God and apply it to our lives.

> **2 Timothy 2:15** (NKJV) [15] Be diligent to present yourself approved to God, a worker who does not need to be ashamed, rightly dividing the word of truth.

God's Word is able to make us strong as Christians.

> **Acts 20:32** (NKJV) [32] "So now, brethren, I commend you to God and to the word of His grace, which is able to build you up and give you an inheritance among all those who are sanctified.

The more we know and obey the Word of God, the more we will mature in God, and the more we will grow in our personal relationship with Jesus.

THE SCRIPTURES HAVE FOUR MAIN FUNCTIONS:

1. ***The Scriptures reveal Jesus Christ (John 5:39).*** The Bible brings God's central word into sharp focus. Jesus is that focus, and He is revealed in the Scriptures.

2. ***The Scriptures build character (John 15:1-4).*** Since the purpose of the vine is to produce fruit, the branches must be pruned in order to ensure a good crop. The Word of God prunes from your life those things that do not bring honor to God. The Word of God hidden in your heart is the key to victory over sin's dominion in your life (Ps. 119:9-11).

3. ***The Scriptures bring spiritual maturity (2 Tim. 3:16-17).*** The Word of God is inspired. This literally means that it is "God-breathed." The Word of God teaches you the right way to live. This is what is referred to as doctrine. The Word of God brings reproof. This means it will show you areas of your life that are wrong. The Word of God brings correction. It helps correct you so that you will walk in obedience to the truth. The Word of God brings instruction. It teaches you how to stay faithful to the truth. The Word of God equips you. It gives you the necessary wisdom and truth to fulfill God's purposes in your life.

4. ***The Scriptures impart faith (Rom. 10:17).*** Without faith, no one can please God (Heb. 11:6). You are called to walk by faith and not by sight (2 Cor. 5:7). Therefore, faith is an essential factor in your relationship with God. Because of the Word of God, you can be a partaker of the divine nature of God (2 Pet. 1:3-4). Everything about God's Word is full of life! It teaches, corrects, guides and trains. It addresses every area of life and is relevant to all people and cultures. God's Word is true; it never fails.

God's Word is light, illuminating the mind and heart to the truth of the Gospel. God's Word is like water, cleansing from sin. Like precious seed, God's Word will bear fruit. When necessary, God's Word purges like fire and breaks like a hammer. God's Word is sweet, bringing healing and nourishment.

God's Word reveals Jesus, and as you come to know Him better, you will be transformed into His image. The Word of God matures you and shapes your character, ever challenging you to become more like the Savior. The Word of God releases faith in your heart, so that you can please God and become a partaker of His nature.

JESUS IS THE "WORD OF GOD"

In many places, the Bible calls itself the "Word of God":

> **1 Thessalonians 2:13** (NKJV) [13] For this reason we also thank God without ceasing, because when you received the word of God which you heard from us, you welcomed *it* not *as* the word of men, but as it is in truth, the word of God, which also effectively works in you who believe.

> **2 Timothy 3:16** (NKJV) [16] All Scripture *is* given by inspiration of God, and *is* profitable for doctrine, for reproof, for correction, for instruction in righteousness,

Jesus is also called the "Word of God":

> **John 1:1** (NKJV) [1] In the beginning was the Word, and the Word was with God, and the Word was God.

> **John 1:14** (NKJV) [14] And the Word became flesh and dwelt among us, and we beheld His glory, the glory as of the only begotten of the Father, full of grace and truth.

Revelation 19:13 (NKJV) [13] He *was* clothed with a robe dipped in blood, and His name is called The Word of God.

Jesus and His Word agree. They agree so perfectly that Jesus, Himself, is called the "Word of God". The Bible is the written Word of God; Jesus is the personal Word of God. The Bible perfectly reveals Jesus; Jesus perfectly fulfills the Bible. The same Holy Spirit who inspired the Word of God reveals Jesus to us through the Word.

Therefore, the more we know and obey the Word of God, the more we will grow in our personal relationship with Jesus. So, if we want to know Jesus more, let us seek Him in His Word.

This, then, is how we build on the foundation of Christ in our lives: through His Word; through hearing and obeying His Word. Paul in writing to the Romans (Rom. 2:17-29), questioned their relationship to God because they were the custodians of the Word and yet not obeying what they were teaching. This is a trap that any of us can fall into!

THE IMPORTANCE OF THE WORD OF GOD

Many Scriptures speak of the importance of the Word of God. It is said that those who attend to the Word hold fast to the Lord and to eternal life (1 Tim. 4:16; 1 John 2:24-25; 2 John 9) while those who leave the Word forsake the Lord (1 Cor. 15:1-2; 2 Tim. 2:16-18; 2 Peter 3:15-17; 2 John 9).

The church of God is called "the pillar (Greek = prop, support) and foundation (Greek = stay, undergirding, from verb: to make stable, settle firmly) of the truth" (1 Tim. 3:15). Much of the modern church has become disobedient in teaching and upholding God's truth.

We are commanded by God to seek doctrinal purity (Phil. 1:27; 2 Tim.

2:15; cf. vv. 19-21) and to keep the church free from error (Rom. 16:17; 1 Tim. 1:3-4; Tit. 1:9-11; Jude 3). This is one of the reasons that the requirements for elders in the church include the ability to teach.

If we live in "truth", we will walk in fellowship with Him who is Truth, and we will love Him with all our heart, soul, mind and strength. Moreover, we will seek to know Him in the fullest way possible, with our minds as well as our spirit.

What we believe will directly influence how we live (Philippians 1:9-11; Colossians 1:9-10). As we know His will, we will be enabled by His Spirit to "walk worthy of the Lord" and to please Him. Ignorance is neither pleasing to God nor profitable to man (1Timothy 1:5; cf. vv. 3-4).

Doctrine is not just academic. Theology breeds methodology. What we believe will greatly affect every aspect of our lives – for better or for worse. Correct theology will be expressed in holy, fruitful living. Sloppy theology will be evidenced by a careless, vain life.

A lack of truth is not simply a void. It is the presence of error. To those who believe doctrine is unimportant, let us say that in reality everyone believes one doctrine or another. If we fail to believe correct doctrine, we have by default embraced incorrect, or at least sloppy, doctrine. Even in wanting to escape doctrine to be open-minded or in wanting to believe that doctrine is unimportant to Christianity, we are practicing a particular doctrine.

PROOF OF OUR LOVE FOR HIM

Since Jesus and His Word agree, if we love Jesus, we will love His Word. If we are truly submitted to Jesus' Lordship in our lives, then we will obey His Word. Thus, our obedience to the Word of God is outward evidence of our inward love for Jesus Christ.

1 John 2:4-5 (NKJV) [4] He who says, "I know Him," and does not keep His commandments, is a liar, and the truth is not in him. [5] But whoever keeps His word, truly the love of God is perfected in him. By this we know that we are in Him.

When John speaks of the love of God being perfected in this verse, he is referring to your love for God. When you obey His Word, your love for Him is mature. This verse reveals the truth that your attitude towards God's Word is your attitude towards God. You do not love God more than your love for His Word. You do not love God more than you obey His Word.

How much does God's Word mean to you? That is how much God means to you. How much do you love and obey His Word? That is how much you love Jesus. There are many people in the world who call themselves Christians, and yet, they do not diligently learn and obey God's Word.

The measure of our love for God's Word, as we obey it, is truly the measure of our love for God. Consider the words of Jesus:

> **John 14:21-23** (NKJV) [21] He who has My commandments and keeps them, it is he who loves Me. And he who loves Me will be loved by My Father, and I will love him and manifest Myself to him." [22] Judas (not Iscariot) said to Him, "Lord, how is it that You will manifest Yourself to us, and not to the world?" [23] Jesus answered and said to him, "If anyone loves Me, he will keep My word; and My Father will love him, and We will come to him and make Our home with him.

This verse reveals several things.

1. *Firstly, if we love Jesus, we will love and obey His Word.* If we do not obey the Word of God, it only reveals that we do not truly love Jesus, no matter how much we say we love Him and no

matter how often we go to church.

2. *Secondly, Jesus manifests Himself to us as we believe and obey His Word.*

3. *Thirdly, the Father and the Son come in a greater measure to our lives, revealing themselves and manifesting themselves to us, as we obey God's Word.*

This is a remarkable promise that as we love and obey Jesus, He will increasingly manifest Himself to us. That means our personal relationship with Him will grow and mature.

The Greek word that is translated *"manifest"* in these verses means *"to physically and outwardly present one's self to the sight of another"*.

> **John 14:19** (NKJV) [19] "A little while longer and the world will see Me no more, but you will see Me. Because I live, you will live also.

The word is used here to refer to an inward revelation of the presence of Christ, and obviously the revelation is a very real one. It is not some abstract and judicial theory that is in view here, but a real experience of fellowship with God.

This experience is not promised to anyone who merely identifies with Jesus or with His church, but only to those who truly love Him and obey His Word. To those who will abandon all for Christ and surrender to Him entirely, this is a precious promise indeed: a promise of the abiding (that is, continuous) and manifest (that is, directly and personally experienced) presence and fellowship of God.

The experience of the presence of God should not be confined to times of special prayer or church meetings; it can be our daily and continuous possession. Jesus wants to make His abode with us. Moment by moment let us draw near to possess Him through meditating in His Word and through believing and obeying His Word.

CHAPTER 3

THE HEBREW STATE

"DULL OF HEARING"

Hebrews 5:11-14 (NKJV) [11] of whom we have much to say, and hard to explain, since you have become dull of hearing. [12] For though by this time you ought to be teachers, you need *someone* to teach you again the first principles of the oracles of God; and you have come to need milk and not solid food. [13] For everyone who partakes *only* of milk *is* unskilled in the word of righteousness, for he is a babe. [14] But solid food belongs to those who are of full age, *that is,* those who by reason of use have their senses exercised to discern both good and evil.

The writer to the Hebrews reveals their state of being which was similar to the Corinthian church.

- Vs. 11 (WEY) *"Since you have become (have grown – Moffit) so dull of apprehension."* He is saying you have become *dull in the ears*. You have become sluggish, having lost momentum. You have become apathetic or dormant, being dead in the water. We are constantly "becoming" something. The Hebrews had "become" in the wrong direction. Instead of growing through a developing apprehension of the truth, they had regressed to the point of disinterest. This is certainly subnormal, whatever else it may be.

- Vs. 12 (Moffit) *"By this time you should be teaching other people, but you still need someone to teach you once more the ELEMENTARY BEGINNINGS of GOD'S LESSONS and need again to be fed with 'MILK' instead of with 'SOLID FOOD'."* They had been 20 to 30 years professing Christ. God counts time! They must look to their foundations and, as seem necessary, review the meaning and implications of those foundations.

- Vs. 13 (NEB) *"Anyone who lives on MILK, BEING AN INFANT, does NOT KNOW what is RIGHT."* Another translation states "Everyone who is limited to milk is 'unskilled'". This is experiential. Infants don't know, and are not expected to know, how to make mature judgments. The tragedy: These were not infants, in terms of time they were adults, but in their behavior they were babies!

- Vs. 14 (NEB) *"But GROWN MEN can take SOLID FOOD; their PERCEPTIONS are TRAINED by long use TO DISCRIMINATE between GOOD and EVIL."* Babies put anything in their mouths. Christians who "grow up into Christ" make decisions concerning right and wrong that infants cannot make.

SOMETHING IS WRONG – THE DISEASE CALLED "DULLNESS OF HEARING"

The writer of Hebrews hasn't come right out and said it until now. But he has implied it. There is something wrong with the Christians he is writing to.

1. In **Hebrews 2:1** he said, *"Pay close attention to the message you've heard lest you drift away.*

2. In **Hebrews 3:1** he said, *"Consider Jesus."*

3. In **Hebrews 3:8** he said, *"Don't harden your hearts like Israel did in the wilderness."*

4. In **Hebrews 3:12** he said, *"Take care, lest you have an evil heart of unbelief."*

5. In **Hebrews 4:1** he said, *"Fear, lest you fail to enter God's rest."*

6. In **Hebrews 4:11** he said, *"Be diligent to enter God's rest lest you fall by disobedience."*

7. In **Hebrews 4:14** he said, *"Hold fast to your confession."*

In all these urgent admonitions you begin to get the impression: this writer is really concerned about some situation in the churches of his day.

- But until now he has only given the cure, not the diagnosis. Now he tells what's wrong.

He comes to the end of the test in 5:9-10 and says that Christ has been perfected through suffering and that He has been designated a High Priest according to the order of Melchizedek. And he takes a breath – you can almost hear him sigh – and says in 5:11,

> "Concerning him [or concerning this – what I've just been talking about briefly] we have much to say, and it is hard to explain, since *you have become dull of hearing*."

And there is our first explicit diagnosis. Here's the disease he is working on in this letter: dullness of hearing.

This is what's behind all those exhortations: Pay close attention! Consider! Don't harden your heart! Fear! Be diligent! Hold fast! These are all doctors' prescriptions for the disease of *dullness of hearing*.

The most urgent question this morning is: Do you have this disease, and if so, how can you get well?

But first we need to make sure we know what he's talking about.

- What is the disease of dullness of hearing?

- Let's let this writer explain his own terms for us: let's take the two words one at a time and look at the one other place in Hebrews where each is used.

"DULLNESS"

Take the first word "dull" or slow or sluggish.

- It's used one other time in the New Testament, namely, in Hebrews 6:12.

Let's read Hebrews 6:11-12 and you will see what the opposite of dullness is,

> "We desire that each one of you show the same *diligence so as to realize the full assurance of hope* until the end, that you may not be sluggish [there's the word for "dull" in our text], but imitators of those through faith and patience inherit the promises."

The opposite of dullness is diligence or eagerness to turn the message of hope into the assurance of hope; it's the imitation of people who hear the promises of God and then respond with faith and patience.

- So dull hearing doesn't mean there is anything wrong with our physical ears. It means there is something wrong with our heart.

- The heart is not eager and diligent to embrace the promises and turn them into faith and patience.

- Instead, the Word comes into the ears and goes down to the heart and hits something hard or tough – or starting to get hard.

- That's dullness of hearing. The promises come to the ear, but there is no passion for them, no lover's embrace, no cherishing or treasuring; and so no faith and no patience and – if things don't change – no inheritance of eternal life.

- This is why the writer of Hebrews wrote this book, and why I exhort you. It is an incredibly dangerous disease, this dullness of hearing.

"HEARING"

The other word we can track down is the word "hearing." It's used one other time in Hebrews, just like "dullness" is, namely, in 4:2.

"For indeed we have had good news preached to us, just as they also; but the word they heard [literally: "the word of hearing – same word as in 5:11, "dull of hearing"] – the word of hearing – did not profit them, because it was not united by faith in those who heard."

So here is the same problem again: a word of good news – a word of God's promise, and a hearing, but no faith.

- This is "dullness of hearing." The word goes in the ears, and comes to the heart, and meets dullness and slowness and hardness.

- The opposite of dullness of hearing is hearing with faith which produces obedience.

You can see this three verses earlier in Hebrews 3:18-19. "And to whom did He [God] swear that they should not enter His rest, but to those who were *disobedient* [note the word!]? And so we see that they were not able to enter because of *unbelief*."

31

- Notice the switch from "disobedient" to "unbelief." I think this means that the root of all disobedience is unbelief – lack of trust in the promises of God.

So you can see what dullness of hearing is and why it is so important. It is a kind of hearing with the ears that is unresponsive in the heart. It doesn't embrace the Word of God with faith, and therefore, it doesn't produce the fruit of patience and obedience. So, whichever way you go – looking at the word "dullness" in 6:12, or looking at the word "hearing" in the context of 4:2, the answer is the same.

"Dullness of hearing" is hearing without faith and without the moral fruit of faith. It's hearing the Bible or the preaching of the Bible the way you hear the freeway noise on I-195, or the way you hear music in the dentist's office or the way you hear recorded warnings at the airport that this is a smoke-free facility. You do but you don't. You have grown dull to the sound. It does not awaken or produce anything.

A word of Jesus from Luke 8:18 is very important here. When He had finished telling the parable of the four soils where the seed is the Word, He says,

> "Therefore *take care how you hear*; for whoever has, to him shall *more* be given; and whoever does not have, even what he thinks he has shall be taken away from him."

In other words, if you have the grace to hear (with faith and fruit), you will get more grace; but if you do not, even what you think you have will be taken away – namely, the Word.

Now I plead with you even now at this point in your reading to be diligent and earnest in how you hear. Lazy, drifting, passive – dull – listening is incredibly dangerous, even now, at this very minute.

Now Jesus' point is the same point the writer to the Hebrews is trying to make:

- The one who has grace to hear will receive more grace, and the one who does not (in other words, is dull or hard in his hearing), even what he thinks he has will be taken away.

Hebrews 5:11 says that there is so much more that the writer wants to give his readers:

> "Concerning him we have much to say ... but you have become dull of hearing."

If they had more grace to hear, they would receive more that the writer has to give. But they are becoming hard and dull, and in danger of throwing away the little they have.

WHAT IS THE REMEDY?

That's the disease. Now what about the remedy? How do you get well? Somebody might object that I am using the term "disease" when the text uses the terms "babe" and "mature." A person who is dull of hearing is compared to a babe (in verse 13b) that has to drink milk. There is nothing diseased about a baby's dependence on milk. So why do I use the image of disease? My answer to this objection is that if a person is still a baby when he is old enough to be a teenager, he has a disease. And the disease in this text is called "dullness of hearing."

So my question remains: what is the remedy?

- Why are some Christians stuck at the baby stage of development with the disease of "dullness of hearing" and what is the cure?

Now keep in mind what dullness of hearing is.

- It's not a physical problem. Deaf people can be the sharpest hearers and blind people can be the sharpest seers. It's not physical.

- Dullness of hearing, you remember from Hebrews 6:12 and 3:18, is the failure to make use of the Word heard to nurture faith and bear the fruit of obedience.

- Dull hearing is passive and lazy and does not reach out and grasp the promises of God and embrace them.

- Passivity produces perpetual babies, who may discover that they are doll-Christians and not living Christians at all. That's the disease.

BECOME MATURE WITH MILK

The key verse to describe the remedy is verse 14:

"Solid food is for the mature, who because of practice have their senses trained to discern good and evil."

Now ask yourself this question: If solid food is only palatable-digestible-for the mature, with what food do you become mature so that you can then eat the solid food? The answer is milk. You become mature with milk.

The problem with these Christians is not that milk is weak or that babes can't eat steak. The problem is that babes are not exercising with the milk they have.

You see the key word there in verse 14: you become mature by "practice" or exercise or habitual responses to the milk.

The problem is that the milk of the Word is not producing muscle of faith. And the muscle of faith is not producing acts of righteousness. This is how you grow from a baby Christian to a mature Christian: from the milk of the Word to the muscle of faith to acts of righteousness.

But note that in verse 14 it doesn't say that the milk of the Word should produce new muscle; it says, in effect, that milk should produce a *new mind* – the mind that can discern between good and evil.

> "Because of practice [the mature] have their senses [internal, moral – spiritual senses] trained to discern good and evil."

Now this is amazing. Don't miss it. It could save you years of wasted living. What verse 14 is saying is that if you want to become mature and understand the more solid teachings of the Word, then the rich, nutritional, precious milk of God's gospel promises must transform your mortal senses – your spiritual mind – so that you can discern between good and evil.

Or let me put it another way. Getting ready to feast on all God's Word is not first an intellectual challenge; it is first a moral challenge.

- If you want to eat the solid food of the Word, you must exercise your spiritual senses so as to develop a mind that discerns between good and evil.

The startling truth is that, if you stumble over Melchizedek, it may be because you watch questionable TV programs.

- If you stumble over the doctrine of election, it may be because you still use some shady business practices.

- If you stumble over the God-centered work of Christ in the cross, it may be because you love money and spend too much and give too little.

The pathway to maturity and to solid biblical food is not first becoming an intelligent person, but becoming an obedient person.

- What you do with alcohol and sex and money and leisure and food and the computer have more to do with your capacity for solid food than with where you go to school or what books you read.

THE WAY YOU DRINK MILK

What this means is that if you want to grow up and feast on the fullness of God's revelation, you don't do it by jumping from milk to meat. You do it by the way you drink the milk. The milk has to make you a certain kind of discerning person before you can digest the meat.

This is so important, because in our highly technological society we are prone to think that education – especially intellectual development – is the key to maturity. This text makes clear that it isn't. There are many Ph.D.'s who choke in their spiritual immaturity on the things of God. And there are many less-educated saints who are deeply mature and can feed with pleasure and profit from the deepest things in God's Word.

So the key to maturity (and the remedy for dullness of hearing) is not jumping from milk to meat. The key is the way you drink the milk – what you do with the milk of the Word.

So let me suggest three steps in how to grow with milk to maturity.

1. **First drink in the milk.** That is, you listen to the milk of the Word – the message of God's promises in the gospel. You read them yourself in the Bible and you sit under the preaching and teaching of God's Word-and you give heed. You are earnest and diligent to apply your heart and mind to what is being said. You are not passive and cavalier and indifferent – babes long for milk, and they are incredibly focused when they are thirsty.

2. **Savor and swallow and digest and be satisfied.** This is crucial. If this doesn't happen, the next stage of discernment will not happen. Here is the miraculous spiritual event of loving what once you hated. You love the taste of the milk: "Taste and see that the Lord is good" (Psalm 34:8). When the promises of God and the God of the promises are tasted, the milk satisfies. When it satisfies, it transforms your values and priorities, which leads to Step 3.

3. **With a heart satisfied with God now, discern good and evil.** There are hundreds of decisions that you must make day in and day out which are not spelled out explicitly in the Bible-what to watch on TV, political positions to take, investment strategies, vocation, insurance, retirement, business tactics, where to live, what to drive, whether to own a gun, how to discipline your children, what to wear, where to volunteer, how much to give, etc., etc.

It doesn't take discernment to know what's wrong if you have a list from God. Knowing when to murder and when to steal and when to commit adultery take no discernment if you believe God gave the Ten Commandments, so verse 14 is talking about decisions that are not laid down specifically in a list.

It says that there is such a thing as discernment between good and evil. How does this discernment come? It comes from habitually (by regular practice) nourishing and shaping your spiritual senses (the word in verse 14 doesn't mean physical senses) by the Word of God until the word becomes a "word of righteousness" – a discerning power, a word producing righteousness full of maturity. Discernment is what you do naturally when the milk of God's promises is so savory and so satisfying that it gives you the mind of Christ.

This is the remedy for "dullness of hearing."

- Drink with delight until the desires of your heart are so transformed that you develop a strong discernment of good and evil.

- Then you will be mature and ready for meat.

CHAPTER 4

LET US PRESS ON TO MATURITY

The apostolic mindset is that maturity is necessary for the proper functioning of the Kingdom. Those who do not mature treat carelessly the holiness of God's sovereign purpose. They are where they began at the starting gate, still in the blocks at the starting line while others are well into the race.

CORRECTING A PROBLEM

> **Hebrews 6:1-3** (NKJV) [1] Therefore, leaving the discussion of the elementary *principles* of Christ, let us go on to perfection, not laying again the foundation of repentance from dead works and of faith toward God, [2] of the doctrine of baptisms, of laying on of hands, of resurrection of the dead, and of eternal judgment. [3] And this we will do if God permits.

"Therefore" refers to what precedes. Some changes must be made. The author of Hebrews is stirred, agitated, angry, concerned – he must stimulate them to maturity. He instructs them to leave. This idea of leaving is not severing from or abandoning. Leaving is like:

- The sprout leaves the seed.

- The adult leaves the child.

- Grade 3 leaves grade 2.

- The second chapter leaves the first.

- Higher mathematics leaves lower mathematics.

- The superstructure leaves the foundation.

The elementary instructions are the beginnings of the Christian life, shortly to be called a foundation, the milk of Hebrews 5:13. The first two verses of Hebrews 6, defines what are the "elementary teachings about Christ." They are also called "the foundation." These are the basic doctrines of the Christian faith. They are "foundational" doctrines. Before we can build, we must first have the foundation laid properly.

There is a question we have to ask here. Something doesn't seem to fit. Look back at Hebrews 5:12, "Though by this time you ought to be teachers, you have need again for someone to teach you the elementary principles of the oracles of God." The question is: how does this fit together with Hebrews 6:1 where it says, "Leave the elementary teachings and don't lay a foundation again."? One seems to say you need to be taught the basics again (5:12), and the other seems to say you should not lay the foundation again (6:1). Well, does he or doesn't he want them to lay a foundation of basics again?

I think the answer is something like this: 5:12 says they need teaching about the basics; 6:1 says they should not lay the foundation of the basics again. So evidently there is a difference between the teaching that they need in 5:12 and the laying again of a foundation in 6:1. One they need and one they don't. What's the difference?

I think the teaching they need about the basics (5:12) is how to use these basics for Christ's sake to press on to maturity. But laying a foundation again, I think, implies that they are losing sight of the basics about Christ and are beginning to occupy themselves with Old Testament and Jewish truths that were used as a foundation for presenting and understanding Christ. The writer doesn't want them to go that far back.

Let me explain. In this writer's mind, laying a foundation for the understanding of Christ is different from teaching about how to live in Christ *on the basis* of that foundation. The foundation he has in mind is described in 6:1-2. The striking thing about this list is that it is not distinctively Christian. It is made up of foundational Old Testament and Jewish truths and practices that the readers probably built on when they were converted. The list has three pairs:

1. Pair one: "Repentance from dead works and of faith toward God"

2. Pair two: Instructions about washings, and laying on of hands"

3. Pair three: "The resurrection of the dead, and eternal judgment"

All these are common Old Testament beliefs or current practices among the Jews. When these readers were evangelized and converted, these things, it seems, had been made foundational as a way of helping them understand the work of Christ. Christ is the goal and fulfillment of all these things. So when verse 1 says they should leave the "elementary teachings about Christ" (or literally: "the word of the beginning of Christ"), what I think it means is that they should not occupy themselves so much with the pre-Christian foundational preparations for Christ that they neglect the glory of the gospel and how to use it to grow into maturity and holiness.

That's what they should *not* do. But what, then, does 5:12 mean when it says that they do need "someone to teach [them] the elementary principles of the oracles of God"? How is that different from laying this foundation again – which they should *not* do? I think the answer is that the teaching they *do* need in 5:12 is how to use the basics about Christ to press on to maturity.

In other words, it's what we saw in the last chapter from 5:14 – they need to learn how to take the milk   the basic truths of the gospel – and practice how to grow with it. The need is not to rebuild foundational facts, but to stand on them and live by them. They need to learn how to take basic gospel truth about Christ and use it to become discerning people about good and evil, so that they attain the holiness without which they will not see the Lord (12:14).

Their problem is not lack of foundational knowledge, but lack of fruitfulness in life. Look at 6:7-8. Here is a description of the problem in a word picture:

> "For ground [that refers to the readers] that drinks the rain which often falls upon it [that refers to the truth they have been hearing] and brings forth vegetation useful to those for whose sake it is also tilled, receives a blessing from God; 8 but if it yields thorns and thistles, it is worthless and close to being cursed, and it ends up being burned."

Here's the issue: has the rain (that is, the milk of the Word) produced thorns and thistles, or has it produced useful vegetation? In other words have the readers learned how to use the Word of Christ (the milk) to become discerning between good and evil, or have they been preoccupied with verbal foundation repair and missed the practical point that Christianity is about the moral and spiritual transformation of life?

The writer is hopeful. Verse 9: "Beloved, we are convinced of better things concerning you." They've been dull of hearing and careless in part. But it's not too late. There's hope. But he is not cavalier or absolutely sure what the outcome will be for them. He wants them to be diligent to have the full assurance of hope (6:11) and the faith and patience and holiness that inherits the promises (6:12; 12:14). But he does not say it's automatic. He urges them on.

Verse 1: "Let us press on to maturity." And he adds the great qualifier in verse 3: "This we will do, if God permits."

It is interesting to note that the first doctrine is repentance which is the start of the Christian's new life in Christ, and the last foundational doctrine is eternal judgment. Thus, the entire length of the Christian's life is covered – from time into eternity.

The six foundational doctrines named here are:

1. Repentance from Dead Works

2. Faith toward God

3. Instruction about Baptisms

4. Laying on of Hands

5. Resurrection of the Dead

6. Eternal Judgment

LET US GO ONTO PERFECTION

The idea of perfection (Greek - *teleios*) is to come of full age (Hebrews 5:14) or to maturity. According to Westcot – A man is said to be '*teleios*' who has reached the full maturity of his powers, the full possession of his rights, his '*teleios*', his end... He is '*teleios*' in whom each faculty and gift has found a harmonious development and use, who has fulfilled the destiny of man by attaining the likeness of God (Genesis 1:26)." – [the epistle to the Hebrews, p. 135]

So when the writer says, "Let us go on..." there are two possible translations. "Let us advance to mature manhood" (Weymouth), or "Let us be borne along toward what is mature." Both are correct conceptually and in relation to the analogy of Scripture, combining the divine and human. "Not laying again the foundation..." is to "not lay over and over again the foundation truths" (JBP). If they have been laid, build on them! Don't keep rehearsing them as if they were the sum total truth – they are "beginnings"!

So if the foundations have not been laid, or have been laid inadequately, then correct that! The writer does not (of course) mean to say that his readers must build higher without having secured their foundations. "And advance we will, if God permits us to do so" (vs. 3 – Weymouth). Not only do we need God's enablement, but His permission. God does not permit building superstructure if the foundation specifications have not been met.

God's whole being pulsates with passion that His church may rise to the imperial design. For that accomplishment He has cleansed the church and provided for it, with every resource required for the operation.

CONSEQUENCES OF NOT MATURING IN CHRIST

Hebrews 6:4-12 (NKJV) [4] For *it is* impossible for those who were once enlightened, and have tasted the heavenly gift, and have become partakers of the Holy Spirit, [5] and have tasted the good word of God and the powers of the age to come, [6] if they fall away, to renew them again to repentance, since they crucify again for themselves the Son of God, and put *Him* to an open shame. [7] For the earth which drinks in the rain that often comes upon it, and bears herbs useful for those by whom it is cultivated, receives blessing from God; [8] but if it bears thorns and briers, *it is* rejected and near to being cursed, whose end *is* to be burned. [9] But, beloved, we are confident of better things concerning you, yes, things that accompany salvation, though we speak in this manner. [10] For God *is* not unjust to forget your work and labor of love which you have shown toward His name, *in that* you have ministered to the saints, and do minister. [11] And we desire that each one of you show the same diligence to the full assurance of hope until the end, [12] that you do not become sluggish, but imitate those who through faith and patience inherit the promises.

This is a solemn warning to all who regress. One cannot ignore such language as "near to being cursed" and in the end to "be burned" (v. 8).

[The Corinthian parallel of "burning" is 1 Corinthians 3:15.] Our Lord issues a warning:

> **Luke 9:62** (NKJV) [62] But Jesus said to him, "No one, having put his hand to the plow, and looking back, is fit for the kingdom of God."

A Closing Illustration

> **Luke 6:46-49** (NKJV) [46] "But why do you call Me 'Lord, Lord,' and not do the things which I say? [47] Whoever comes to Me, and hears My sayings and does them, I will show you whom he is like: [48] He is like a man building a house, who dug deep and laid the foundation on the rock. And when the flood arose, the stream beat vehemently against that house, and could not shake it, for it was founded on the rock. [49] But he who heard and did nothing is like a man who built a house on the earth without a foundation, against which the stream beat vehemently; and immediately it fell. And the ruin of that house was great."

These two men are both "comers"; "hearers" and "builders", the difference is at this point. One of them built a proper foundation. The other didn't. When you look at the houses that they built, they might have looked the same. However, there was a difference, only one had a secure foundation which obviously took him a longer to build with a greater cost. The "hearer" in this example settled for cheapness, immediacy, and appearance. The "doer" in contrast, dug deep (Luke 6:48) and "laid the foundation on a rock." He took the time to remove everything between what he was to build and the rock which would form the foundation. He got to the bottom of things. The storms of life are inevitable. No one is exempt from the storms of life whether you are righteous or not. The Scriptures tell us that "Everything must be shaken" (Hebrews 12:25).

There are two dangers that are evident from this example. One could build a true foundation, but no house. Or one could build his house on a faulty foundation. Neither would accomplish the desired purpose. We must build a proper foundation and then go onto maturity by continuing to build upon the foundation that is secure.

CHAPTER 5

REPENTANCE FROM DEAD WORKS

Repentance is essential to constructing a firm foundation in Christ. There is a great difference between true repentance and worldly sorrow, and unfortunately, too many have confused the two. The work of repentance originates from God through the convicting work of the Holy Spirit, but we have a vital role to play in the process, too. A clear understanding of sin and repentance will lay a strong foundation in our lives, and upon it we can build the other vital principles of our faith.

Repentance is not a popular subject, but it is central to the Christian life. The Bible teaches that repentance precedes forgiveness of sins:

> **Acts 2:38** (NKJV) [38] Then Peter said to them, "Repent, and let every one of you be baptized in the name of Jesus Christ for the remission of sins; and you shall receive the gift of the Holy Spirit."

Jesus said that without repentance man will perish in his sins:

> **Luke 13:3** (NKJV) [3] I tell you, no; but unless you repent you will all likewise perish.

THE MEANING OF REPENTANCE

In the Old Testament there are two Hebrew words that are translated "repentance":

- The first one, "*naham*", means to "lament" or "to grieve" and refers to the aroused emotions of God or man when undertaking a different course of action.

- The other word, *"shubh"*, is most generally employed to express the Scriptural idea of genuine repentance. It is used extensively by the prophets and means "a radical change in one's attitude towards sin and God." It implies a conscious moral separation, and a personal decision to forsake sin and enter into fellowship with God.

In the New Testament there are two Greek words that are translated "repentance":

- One of these, *"metamelomai"*, is like the first Old Testament word we considered *"naham"*, and means "to have a feeling or care, concern or regret."

- The other word, *"metanoeo"*, means "to have another mind" and occurs in the noun and verb form 57 times. It is also associated with the word "turn" and "describes that deep and radical change whereby a sinner turns from the idols of sin and self unto God."

OTHER DEFINITIONS OF THE WORD "REPENTANCE":

- "Repentance may be defined as the voluntary change in the mind of the sinner whereby he turns from sin. It involves a change of view, a change of feeling, and a change of purpose." (Pardington)

- "Repentance expresses that mighty change in the mind, heart, and life wrought by the Spirit of God." (Trench)

- "Repentance describes that deep and radical change whereby a sinner turns from the idols of self and sin unto God, and devotes every movement of the inner and outer man to the captivity of His obedience." (Chalmers)

- "Repentance implies an intellectual and a hearty giving up of all controversy with God upon all and every point. It implies a conviction that God is wholly right, and the sinner wholly wrong, and a thorough and hearty abandonment of all excuses and apologies for sin." (Finney)

- "Repentance denotes primarily a change of mind, taking a wiser view of the past, including regret for the ill then done, and leading to a change of life for the better." (L. Berkhof).

We could then make a summarized statement about repentance:

- Repentance is the reforming and changing of the <u>mind</u>, the stirring and directing of the <u>emotions</u> to urge the required change; and the action of the yielded <u>will</u> in turning the whole man away from sin and to God.

THE TRUE GOSPEL ALWAYS INCLUDES THE PREACHING OF REPENTANCE

John the Baptist was Jesus' forerunner, and he preached repentance:

Mark 1:2-4 (NKJV) [2] As it is written in the Prophets: "Behold, I send My messenger before Your face, *Who will prepare Your way before You.*" [3] *"The voice of one crying in the wilderness:* 'Prepare the way of the LORD; *Make His paths straight.*'" [4] John came baptizing in the wilderness and preaching a baptism of repentance for the remission of sins.

Jesus preached repentance:

Mark 1:14-15 (NKJV) [14] Now after John was put in prison, Jesus came to Galilee, preaching the gospel of the kingdom of God, [15] and saying, "The time is fulfilled, and the kingdom of God is at hand. Repent, and believe in the gospel."

Jesus' disciples preached repentance:

Mark 6:12 (NKJV) [12] So they went out and preached that *people* should repent.

Luke 24:46-47 (NKJV) [46] Then He said to them, "Thus it is written, and thus it was necessary for the Christ to suffer and to rise from the dead the third day, [47] and that repentance and remission of sins should be preached in His name to all nations, beginning at Jerusalem.

Paul's message was one of repentance:

Acts 20:20-21 (NKJV) [20] how I kept back nothing that was helpful, but proclaimed it to you, and taught you publicly and from house to house, [21] testifying to Jews, and also to Greeks, repentance toward God and faith toward our Lord Jesus Christ.

God, Himself, "commands all people everywhere to repent" (Acts 17:30)! Without true repentance, any profession of faith will be empty words. Any gospel that leaves out repentance is a false gospel. Any "faith message" that does not equally stress repentance will never work.

THE IMPORTANCE OF REPENTANCE

- God commands it immediately and universally (Acts 17:30).

- Repentance is the reason for Christ's coming (Luke 5:32).

- Repentance is part of our Lord's commission to us (Luke 24:47).

- Repentance is necessary to avoid destruction (Luke 13:3).

- Repentance is necessary to eternal life (Acts 11:18).

- Repentance is necessary for forgiveness (Acts 2:38).

- Repentance is necessary for entrance into the kingdom (Matthew 4:17).

- Repentance is God's desire for all (2 Peter 3:9).

- Repentance is part of the Christian's foundation (Hebrews 6:1).

THE CAUSES OF REPENTANCE

- The goodness of God causes men to repent (Romans 2:4).

- Christ's call causes men to repent (Matthew 9:13).

- Preaching causes men to repent (Matthew 12:41).

- A rebuke causes men to repent (Luke 17:3).

- Godly sorrow causes men to repent (2 Corinthians 7:10).

- The divine gift enables men to repent (Acts 11:18; 5:31; 2 Tim. 2:25).

The Scripture teaches that repentance is a gift of God (Lamentations 5:21; Acts 5:31; Acts 11:18; 2 Timothy 2:24-25). From your side, however, you should not wait until you feel God has given you the gift of repentance, but you should repent as soon as you see the need to do so. From your side, there is nothing stopping you from repenting. The scripture teaches that "now is the time of God's favor, now is the day of salvation" (2 Corinthians 6:2).

A common misconception about repentance is that it is primarily an

emotion. Repentance does involve regret because if you do not regret your sinful way of life with its consequences of death and alienation from God, you will never truly turn from it. However, repentance is more than regret. Repentance is an inward decision to change which results in outward actions of change.

True repentance is a complete about-face in thought and action. First, you change your thinking. There is a new perspective of the nature, awfulness, and consequences of sin. There is recognition that what you are in your natural state is deeply abhorrent to a holy God. Then, you change your actions. You turn from disobedience, selfishness, and rebellion and turn to God. You turn away from sin, submit your life to God, and make Jesus your Lord.

Repentance is not just a mental acceptance of truth or just world sorrow. It is characterized by the following:

Godly sorrow for sin (Ps. 38; 2 Cor. 7:10). True repentance is not just sorrow within or towards other people, but first and foremost, it is true sorrow towards God. When you truly repent, you see sin as God sees it.

After he betrayed Jesus Judas regretted his sins (Matthew 27:3). Nevertheless, Judas did not truly repent, and he was lost eternally (Acts 1:25).

It is possible for people to shed tears when they are under the conviction of sin, when they are caught in their sin, or when they receive the bad consequences of their sin, but never actually to change their mind about their life and receive salvation. True repentance involves change. Repentance is not primarily an emotion but a decision: a decision to turn from sin to serve Jesus.

Paul spoke of the relationship of "godly sorrow" to true repentance in 2 Corinthians 7:10, and the difference between that and false "worldly sorrow" is that " godly sorrow brings repentance that leads to salvation and leaves no regret, but worldly sorrow brings death."

Confession of sin (Ps. 32:5; 1 John 1:9). True repentance confesses the act as sin, not as a mistake or error. It assumes responsibility for the wrongdoing and doesn't blame others.

Willingness to give up sin (Prov. 28:13). True repentance includes the

decision to cease from the sin. If a person is not willing to stop sinning, then he hasn't really repented.

Hatred of sin (Ezek. 20:43-44). True repentance causes the sinner to see how truly awful sin is and to hate it.

Inclusion of restitution (Luke 19:8; Lev. 6:1-7). True repentance attempts to redress any wrongs done. It faces up to the consequences of sin and makes amends where possible.

ESAU AND REPENTANCE

At this point, it would be profitable to examine a verse about Esau that is sometimes misquoted in this regard.

> **Hebrews 12:17** (NKJV) [17] For you know that afterward, when he wanted to inherit the blessing, he was rejected, for he found no place for repentance, though he sought it diligently with tears.

In a careless moment, Esau sold his birthright to his brother Jacob in exchange for a bowl of soup. But later he regretted what he had done, and he went to his father Isaac and with tears tried to obtain the blessing that was once his:

> **Genesis 27:38** (NKJV) [38] And Esau said to his father, "Have you only one blessing, my father? Bless me—me also, O my father!"

And Esau lifted up his voice and wept.

The repentance (or change of mind) that Esau sought was not his own but his father's. He wanted his father to change his mind and take the blessing from Jacob and give it back to him. However, Isaac would not change his mind.

> **Genesis 27:33** (NKJV) [33] Then Isaac trembled exceedingly, and said, "Who? Where *is* the one who hunted game and brought *it* to me? I ate all *of it* before you came, and I have blessed him— *and* indeed he shall be blessed."

Isaac had already given the blessing, and he could not take it back from Jacob.

In this way, Esau "found no place of repentance, though he sought it carefully with tears."

If you do not understand the meaning of this, you may have the picture of Esau trying to repent of his sin but not being able to because God was withholding the gift of repentance from him. However, that is not the case. The repentance (or change of mind) that Esau sought with tears was not his own but his father's.

Although repentance is a gift from God's side, from your side there is nothing stopping you from repenting right now if you need to. So, do not let a misconception about this verse stop you from forsaking sin and coming to God on the basis that you do not think God has given you or even wants to give you the gift of repentance. God is not holding back repentance from you. If you do not repent, it is because you choose not to repent; it is not because God denied you something you wanted.

Remember:

> (God) commands all people everywhere to repent. (Acts 17:30)

That means you are responsible to repent and to get right with God. After you do repent you will look back and realize that God gave you repentance, but prior to repentance, you were only doing what you chose to do.

TRUE REPENTANCE WILL RESULT IN WORKS OF RIGHTEOUSNESS

Repentance is an inward decision that produces outward change. Without the outward change there is doubt the inward decision was ever real.

John the Baptist told those coming to him for baptism to, "Produce fruit in keeping with repentance" (Matthew 3:8). In other words, John told them first to prove that they had repented by their good works, and then come to his baptism. Outward works prove the genuineness of inward repentance.

Paul preached the same kind of repentance – a repentance that is not just words, but one that results in works (Acts 26:20).

EVIDENCES ASSOCIATED WITH REPENTANCE

Conversion is associated with repentance. Our relationship to God has many aspects. God is infinitely aware of all these simultaneously. Man, however, because of his finiteness, must learn from revelation each aspect, and relate it to every other aspect. Each aspect is a part of the whole, the whole being necessary for a healthy Christian life. Paul called it "the whole counsel of God" (Acts 20:27).

Repentance and conversion are inseparable. The Greek word translated "convert" is "*epistrepho*." "It denotes not merely a change of the mind, but stresses the fact that a new relationship is established, that the active life is made to move in another direction" (Berkhof). "The sinner consciously forsakes the old sinful life and turns to a life in communion with and devoted to God" (Berkhof).

- Conversion is necessary for entrance into the Kingdom of God (Matthew 18:3).

- Conversion saves us from death (James 5:20).

- Conversion was the burden of the Apostles (Acts 26:18-20).

- Conversion is necessary for blotting out sin (Acts 3:19).

Conversion involves:

- Acknowledging the Divine Lordship (Luke 1:16; Acts 9:35; 11:21; 15:19).

- Turning "from darkness to light."

- Turning "from the power of Satan unto God" (Acts 26:18).

- Turning from the "vanities" of "idolatry" (Acts 14:15; 1 Thess. 1:9).

Christians can experience conversion (Luke 22:32).

Repentance and conversion are illustrated in the story of the prodigal son (Luke 15:11-32). After the son had wasted all his substance and been reduced to the humiliation of the "pig pen," he made a quality, inward decision to turn in a different direction:

> **Luke 15:18** (NKJV) [18] I will arise and go to my father, and will say to him, "Father, I have sinned against heaven and before you,

That inward decision then resulted in outward action:

Luke 15:20 (NKJV) [20] "And he arose and came to his father. But when he was still a great way off, his father saw him and had compassion, and ran and fell on his neck and kissed him.

And his father responded graciously to his true repentance. This is a wonderful picture of the sinner's true repentance and turning to God, and God's resulting acceptance of him!

Faith is associated with repentance (Mark 1:15; Acts 20:21).

Baptism is an accompaniment to repentance (Acts 2:38).

Works are associated with repentance (Acts 26:20).

Fruits are associated with repentance (Matthew 3:8).

CHRISTIANS DO REPENT

Whenever there is sin, there must be repentance. In the Corinthian church, Paul taught that their sorrow must lead to repentance (2 Corinthians 7:9; 12:20-21). So many people tell us they are sorry, but this instruction is saying that the sorrow must lead to change. God is working a process of sanctification in all of us. The question is: are we interested in the minimum requirements or in God's maximum development? Sometimes the church is so interested in converts that she waters down the need for repentance. We need to receive new converts on God's terms.

Repentance is also corporate as well as personal.

- The Christians in Ephesus (Rev. 2:5).

- The Christians in Pergamos (Rev. 2:16).

- The Christians in Sardis (Rev. 3:3).

- The Christians in Laodicea (Rev. 3:19).

"Today cheap grace is being preached and received by cheap faith, resulting in cheap Christians." (Havner)

The Christians of our day are oftentimes intertwined with our relativistic society.

The change wrought in repentance is so deep and radical as to affect the whole spiritual nature and involve the entire personality, including the intellect, the emotions and the will.

Intellect. Repentance is that change of a sinner's mind that leads him or her to turn from evil ways and live. Intellectually, human beings must apprehend sin as unutterably heinous, the divine law as perfect and binding, and themselves as falling short of the requirements of a holy God.

Emotions. It is possible to have a knowledge of sin without abhorring it as something that dishonors God and ruins humanity: the change of view may lead only to a dread of punishment and not to the hatred and abandonment of sin (Ex. 9:27; Num. 22:34; 1 Sam. 15:24; Matt. 27:4). A change in emotional attitude is necessarily involved in genuine repentance. A penitent cannot be emotionally indifferent to sin. Before there can be a hearty turning away from unrighteousness, there must be a consciousness of sin's effect on humanity and its offensiveness to God. While sorrow for sin is not equivalent to repentance, it may be a powerful impulse to a genuine turning from sin. But the type of grief that issues in repentance must be distinguished from that which simply plunges into remorse. There is a godly sorrow and a worldly sorrow: the former brings life, the latter brings death (Matt. 27:3-5; Luke 18:33; 2 Cor. 7:9). True repentance involves not only a conviction of personal sinfulness, but also an earnest appeal to God to forgive according to His mercy (Psalm 51:1, 10-14).

Will. The most prominent element in the psychology of repentance is the volitional. The demand for repentance clearly implies human free will and individual responsibility, but it is equally clear that God is represented as taking the initiative in repentance. This paradox reflects the mysterious relationship between the human and the divine personalities. God will accept no external substitute for the necessary internal change. Sackcloth for the body and remorse for the soul are not to be confused with a determined abandonment of sin and a return to God. Not material sacrifice, but a spiritual change, is the inexorable demand of God (Psalm 51:17; Isa. 1:1; Jer. 6:20; Hos. 6:6).

WHAT IS THE ROLE OF FORGIVENESS IN THE PROCESS?

Repentance does not stand alone; forgiveness is its spiritual companion. After you have realized your sinful condition in the presence of God's holiness, you need to experience the greatness of God's love and mercy. God gave His only Son so that you might have forgiveness. It cost Him dearly, but that shows how much He loves you (1 John 1:7-9).

All heaven is made glad when sinners repent. There is a great celebration in heaven when one man or woman repents of sin and turns to God. In Luke 15:7 and 10, the Bible speaks of this great rejoicing over repentant sinners.

Repentance brings pardon and forgiveness. Apart from repentance, the prophets and apostles spoke of no other way of securing pardon (Isa. 55:7; Acts 3:19). Self-help, good thoughts, being good, or any of the other countless ways people try to atone for wrongdoing cannot bring forgiveness; only repentance brings spiritual forgiveness for sin.

The Holy Spirit is poured upon those who repent and turn to Christ. "Repent... and you shall receive the gift of the Holy Spirit" (Acts 2:38). Impenitence prevents the full coming of the Spirit into the heart. "Do you show contempt for the riches of His kindness, tolerance and patience, not realizing that God's kindness leads you towards repentance?" (Romans 2:4)

SUMMARY

Because of the Fall, sin is part of human life. Sin displeases God and separates us from Him. To be forgiven of sin, we must first repent of it. Repentance means much more than feeling sorry for sin. It includes confession of wrongdoing, willingness to give up the sin, conscious turning from it, and acceptance of Jesus' sacrificial death as atonement. True repentance brings pardon, forgiveness, and restoration. All heaven is made glad when even one sinner repents!

With repentance set firmly in place in our foundation, we are secure in God. What we learned in coming to Him must also remain as a foundation stone for us to grow in Him as well. Repentance remains for us something to turn to for the transformation of our lives as we agree with the Word of God and allow Him to transform us into His likeness.

CHAPTER 6

FAITH TOWARDS GOD

Faith towards God is a natural progression following repentance from dead works. In repentance, the focus is on self and the need to come clean before a holy God, but faith moves the focus from self to God.

Dead works always interfere with faith towards God, and anything apart from faith in God is dead (Heb. 11:6; Rom. 14:23). Without faith, we will not even come to Him. Without faith, nothing in our lives will be acceptable to God. We may perform many religious acts, but without faith, none of it will please God; our whole life will be "sin" in His eyes. We must turn from dead works before we can ever turn to God. Only then can faith towards God develop.

Faith, in context of this foundational truth, can be defined as "having trust, assurance, or confidence in another person and that person's word." Having faith in God involves an exchange of trust from self to Him.

The root word from which we get "faith" (noun) and "believe" (verb), and its derivative are found in the New Testament 619 times.

The word **"faith"** (Greek word – *pistis*) can be defined faith, belief, firm persuasion, assurance, firm conviction, honesty, integrity, faithfulness and truthfulness.

The word **"believe"** (Greek word – *pisteuo*) means to trust in, put faith in, confide in, rely on a person or thing; having a mental persuasion; to entrust, commit to the charge or power of.

> "It is the act by which a person lays hold on God's preferred resources, becomes obedient to what God prescribes, and

abandoning all self-interest, and self-reliance, trust God completely." – W. A. Whitehouse

"It is a receiving of Christ for just what He is representing to be in His gospel, and an unqualified surrender of the will, and of the whole being to Him." – Finney

THE BIBLICAL DEFINITION OF "FAITH"

Faith is one of the few terms specifically defined in the Bible:

Hebrews 11:1 (NKJV) [1] Now faith is the substance [assurance] of things hoped for, the evidence of things not seen. For by it the elders obtained a good report [God's approval]. Through faith we understand that the worlds were framed by the word of God [He spoke and it was], so that the things which are seen were not made of things which do appear."

Faith links us with God and is the assurance that the revealed things promised in the future are true, and that the unseen things are real! Faith is certain that what it believes is true, and that what it expects will come. It is not the hope that looks forward with wistful longing; it is the hope that looks forward with utter certainty. Hope is an expectancy concerning things in the future, whereas faith is a "substance," based upon our future hope that we possess now. It is not the hope which takes refuge in perhaps; it is the hope which is founded on a conviction. The future and the unseen can be made real for men by faith.

True faith is in the heart (Rom. 10:10). It is more than merely agreeing with truth. It involves a heart receiving and submitting to that truth. One cannot be saved without faith (Mark 16:16; Luke 8:12; 1 Cor. 1:21; Eph. 2:8). One cannot please God without faith (Heb. 11:6).

How does Faith towards God Develop?

Faith develops when you have the right attitude. Faith is a persuasion. The word faith comes from the Greek word *pistis*, which means "firm persuasion," "strong and welcome belief," or "the conviction of the truth of anything" (see 2 Tim. 1:12). Before your faith can develop, you need to realize the futility of everything apart from God. Faith involves an attitude of humility and submission to the will of God (Phil. 2:5-8), and you need to confess this attitude.

Faith grows as you acknowledge its substance and reality. Faith is not imagination or the wishing of things into being. It is the conviction of the truth by the inner working of the Holy Spirit. If God gives you the faith for something, you can be sure that in the mind of God that thing really exists and belongs to you already (Heb. 11:1; Num. 23:19).

Faith develops as you understand that it is a gift from God. You cannot work yourself up into believing. It is not the result of mental gymnastics. The Holy Spirit must place the ability to believe God within your heart (Eph. 2:8).

Faith also develops through your knowledge of God. You cannot trust someone you do not know. The more you know God and understand His faithfulness, His love, His character, His ways, and His greatness, the more you will be able to trust Him. This is the basis for true faith towards God (Deut. 7:9; Ps. 9:10; 1 Thess. 5:24). You get to know God and thus trust Him as the Holy Spirit reveals Him through the Scriptures and as you, by faith, prove Him through life's experiences (Heb. 11:6). You cannot really get to know someone unless you speak to him. Therefore, prayer, which is speaking to God, is a wonderful means of getting to know God. Prayer always manifests two things: first, a heart-desire that all you do is in the will of God and second, a confession of your total dependence on Him. Remember: God's faithfulness is great and unfailing (Ps. 89:34), and you need to magnify His faithfulness (Ps. 92:1-2; Ps. 89:1).

Faith develops as a response to hearing. God communicates His thoughts through His Word. When He enables you to hear what He is saying by the Spirit, this creates within you the response of believing, or being persuaded that what He is saying is indeed true. "Faith comes by hearing, and hearing by the [specific] word of God" (Rom. 10:17).

As you confess the word of faith given to you, and when appropriate, act on it, you will find the creative power of God working in and through that word to bring it to pass. Jesus says that by faith nothing shall be impossible (Matt. 17:20). Having faith involves an exchange from relying on only one source of knowledge (sense knowledge) to relying on a higher source of knowledge (revelation knowledge).

Sense knowledge is all knowledge that is perceived through the five senses. It is limited knowledge and is described as the wisdom of man (1 Cor. 2:4-6). Revelation knowledge, in contrast, is based upon a higher source, the Word of God. It is revealed by the Holy Spirit to the spirit of man, and it is described as the wisdom of God (1 Cor. 2:7-16).

"Now faith is the assurance (the confirmation, the title-deed) of the things (we) hope for, being the proof of things (we) do not see and the convictions of their reality – faith perceiving as real fact what is not revealed to the senses" (Heb. 11:1 AMP).

Faith develops through experiencing God and His faithfulness. The more you have faith towards God, the more you experience His faithfulness, and consequently, the more your faith grows. God has also given gifts of healing, miracles, and other gifts to point you to Him and increase your faith (see John 2:11; 11:15).

Faith grows as you remember God's past faithfulness. When you remember what God did for you yesterday, you will have faith to believe he will take care of you tomorrow. "Jesus Christ is the same yesterday, today, and forever" (Heb. 13:8).

What Faith is Not!

Faith is not mental assent. Since faith is in the heart, it is important to understand the profound difference between faith and mental assent. Many Christians theoretically "believe" in Jesus. They agree with the doctrine of the Bible. Intellectually they concur with the truths of Christianity, but their "head faith" produces no change in their lives.

Faith, on the other hand, has "substance" – spiritual dynamic and reality – to it. It will change your life from head to toe, and it will give you assurance right now. If your Christianity is merely "head faith," you will not possess assurance of your salvation or of any of the other promises of God. Faith has spiritual "substance"; it is not just mentally agreeing with the doctrines of the Bible.

Faith is not sight. "We live by faith, not by sight" (2 Corinthians 5:7). Paul contrasts faith and sight in this verse. To "live by sight," means that your life is dominated and controlled by what you see and feel in the natural world around you.

To live by faith, on the other hand, means that you live according to the written Word of God. If we live by sight, we will live according to only what our natural senses tell us, but if we live by faith in God, we will put His Word as a higher authority than what we see and feel. To the spiritual man, sight comes after faith, not before it. Consider the words of David:

> **Psalm 27:13** (NKJV) [13] *I would have lost heart,* unless I had believed That I would see the goodness of the LORD In the land of the living.

In the midst of very difficult circumstances, David believed the promises of God rather than being overwhelmed by his apparently hopeless situation. Because of his faith, his circumstances later changed, but his faith came first: he "believed to see."

Jesus taught that faith comes first and sight comes second:

> **John 11:40** (NKJV) [40] Jesus said to her, "Did I not say to you that if you would believe you would see the glory of God?"

If you can already see a thing, you do not need faith to believe it. You need faith to believe what you cannot see or feel. Many immature Christians only believe what they see, but the mature Christian will see what he believes (when he believes the Word of God).

There are a number of examples in the Bible of men and women who chose to walk by faith in the Word of God rather than according to the evidence of their feelings or circumstances.

Abraham: (Romans 4:17-21)

There is one man in the Bible who is referred to as "the father of all them that believe" (Romans 4:11) and "the father of us all" (Romans 4:16). His name is Abraham. Christians are those who "walk in the steps of that faith of our father Abraham" (Romans 4:12), and are spoken of as "the children of Abraham" (Gal. 3:7; 3:29).

When Paul wanted to illustrate saving, justifying faith, he recounted Abraham's relationship to God. The manner in which Abraham manifested faith is the manner in which we must manifest faith.

We find Paul's reference to Abraham's faith in Romans 4:

- "He turned from his hopeless condition" (Romans 4:18-19).

- "He embraced the hope expressed in the divine promise" (Romans 4:18).

- "He didn't waver in his commitment" (Romans 4:20).

- "He rejoiced in the Word as the accomplished fact" (Romans 4:20).

We could also express that Abraham did these 3 things:

1. He believed the promise of God that he would have a son.

2. He disregarded the physical evidence before him that was contrary to the promise of God.

3. He held fast to his faith, and in the end saw the promise of God come to pass.

Mary: (Luke 1:34-38)

Mary believed the Word of God despite impossibility of the promise. For that reason, God commended her by His Spirit in Elizabeth (Luke 1:45). You, too, will be commended by God when you believe the promises of His Word in the face of impossible circumstances.

Peter: (Luke 4:4-6)

In spite of the apparent foolishness of Jesus' instructions, Peter believed His Word and let down the net. Look at the result!

THE DIFFERENCE BETWEEN FAITH AND PRESUMPTION

We must point out that the kind of faith that works is only faith in God based upon His Word. "Faith" will not work when it is not based upon God's promise. Furthermore, even faith in God's promises will not work when the conditions for receiving those promises are not met.

Moreover, a living faith in God is born out of a living relationship with

Him. Faith is not real at all unless it is the spontaneous consequence of a personal relationship with the Faithful One; not out of guilt, nor constraint, nor perceived religious duty, but simply the natural result of a sincere fellowship of love with God.

We will only really trust one whom we know. Those who know God will put their trust in Him.

> **Psalm 9:10** (NKJV) [10] And those who know Your name will put their trust in You; For You, LORD, have not forsaken those who seek You.

We will only be able to truly put our trust in the Lord, if we have first drawn near to Him.

> **Psalm 73:28** (NKJV) [28] But *it is* good for me to draw near to God; I have put my trust in the Lord GOD, That I may declare all Your works.

If our religion is mostly theoretical and we lack a personal relationship with Jesus, then we will never be able to trust Him no matter how many times we exhort each other that faith in God is our obligation and responsibility. The true Christian life is not that we must try to trust Him; it is that through His gracious self-revelation and His indwelling life we may trust Him, and we are enabled to trust Him.

Remember, there is a world of difference between head faith and heart faith. Head faith is presumption; heart faith is based upon the Word of God that is in the heart of the believer who is walking in daily fellowship with and has heart obedience to God. Head faith will fail; heart faith will bear genuine and lasting fruit.

Places where you can misplace your faith:

- In weapons (Psalm 44:6)

- In wealth (Luke 12:21)

- In oppression or extortion (Psalm 62:10

- In human greatness (Psalm 146:3)

- In one's self (Proverbs 28:26)

- In idols (Isaiah 42:17)

- In false prophets (Jer. 7:4, 8)

THE ATTRIBUTES OF FAITH

Faith is an action word. It empowers. It produces. It attracts. It is the savor of the salt, the light on the candle that will pierce the darkness. Faith is the power that moves mountains.

We who claim to be His are to live by such faith! We are to win the world through such faith! As we have already expressed, without faith we cannot please God (Heb. 11:6). The whole range and reach and rigors and works of faith are central to living in Christ, to living for Christ. Consider, then, the spectrum of faith; the attributes, the dimensions, and requirements of our Christian faith.

Faith trusts. It does not doubt. It does not question God's Word. It embraces His covenant without reluctance or reservation. It places no limit on His Sovereign grace or power (2 Tim. 1:12)

Faith obeys. Faith impels obedience to God, without hesitation, without reservation. It's all-consuming desire is to bring into captivity every thought to obedience to Jesus Christ – walking according to His Word, keeping His law, obeying His commandments (Rom. 6:16; Joshua 24:15).

Faith lives. Faith is dynamic. Those who are faith-full are to be dynamos for Christ – bold but not abrasive, discerning but not contentious, aggressive but not arrogant. Faith does not act unseemly (Rom. 3:8). By faith we seek to live for (and be like) Jesus Christ (Col. 3; Phil 1:20-21).

Faith grows. It matures. It builds; it is not stagnant. It seeks a spiritual fullness through study of God's Word and through increasingly yielding to Him and His law-Word, His will, and His purpose (Col. 3:16-17).

Faith empowers. It strengthens. Faith does not surrender the world to Satan or any of his magistrates; it has not abdicated His sovereignty! Faith is the power to overcome all obstacles in the service of the King. Faith provides the inner backbone and that outward courage to withstand the hatred of man and the tempting of Satan (John 1:12).

Faith endures. Faith is constant. It is not on-again, off-again. It has staying power. It perseveres, persists, stands fast, is courageous. The faith-full person keeps his eyes upon Jesus.

Faith attracts. It invites, encourages, is winsome. Faith rejoices. It glorifies God. Those who are faith-full walk as children of God; Jesus said they are the light of the world. We are transformed to be transformers for Him (1 Pet. 3:15).

Faith loves. For there abides faith and hope and love – and faith is a product of love. Those who truly love Jesus truly believe in Jesus! And, if we love Him, we seek to keep His commandments. We love our brothers and sisters in Christ. And more: we love the unlovely and the unlovable even as we love ourselves (Col. 3:12-13).

Faith produces. Faith is not dormant. It manifests itself in works. It bears good fruit. Why? Because those who are faithful, those who hold fast to the faith are branches of the True Vine in which they live and breathe and have their being (James 2:19-20).

THE WORKS OF FAITH (APPLYING THE PRINCIPLE)

Of all the deceits foisted on Christendom, surely one of the most deadly is this: Since we are saved by grace (not works), we need not be concerned with works.

Those who have minimized the importance of good works in the life of the Christian generally refer to the Apostle Paul's letter to the church at Ephesus:

> **Ephesians 2:8-9** (NKJV) [8] For by grace you have been saved through faith, and that not of yourselves; *it is* the gift of God, [9] not of works, lest anyone should boast.

Paul's admonition did not stop there, he went on, and so must we if we are to live by the whole Word of God:

> **Ephesians 2:10** (NKJV) [10] For we are His workmanship, created in Christ Jesus for good works, which God prepared beforehand that we should walk in them.

And, in his letter to Titus, Paul again emphasized that we who are slaves to the Master must understand and apply the essential linkage between salvation and works:

> **Titus 2:13-14** (NKJV) [13] looking for the blessed hope and glorious appearing of our great God and Savior Jesus Christ, [14] who gave Himself for us, that He might redeem us from every lawless deed and purify for Himself *His* own special people, zealous for good works.

> **Titus 3:5-8** (NKJV) [5] not by works of righteousness which we have done, but according to His mercy He saved us, through the washing of regeneration and renewing of the Holy Spirit, [6] whom He poured out on us abundantly through Jesus Christ our Savior, [7] that having been justified by His grace we should become heirs according to the hope of eternal life. [8] This is a faithful saying, and these things I want you to affirm constantly, that those who have

believed in God should be careful to maintain good works. These things are good and profitable to men.

What, then, of that faith which is devoid of works? Is it not a dead and deadly faith – a pernicious force which gives the unsaved person reason to doubt the power and the purpose of the Christian faith? Without a doubt it is!

James 2:26 (NKJV) [26] For as the body without the spirit is dead, so faith without works is dead also.

Matthew 25:31-46 (NKJV) [31] "When the Son of Man comes in His glory, and all the holy angels with Him, then He will sit on the throne of His glory. [32] All the nations will be gathered before Him, and He will separate them one from another, as a shepherd divides *his* sheep from the goats. [33] And He will set the sheep on His right hand, but the goats on the left. [34] Then the King will say to those on His right hand, 'Come, you blessed of My Father, inherit the kingdom prepared for you from the foundation of the world: [35] for I was hungry and you gave Me food; I was thirsty and you gave Me drink; I was a stranger and you took Me in; [36] I *was* naked and you clothed Me; I was sick and you visited Me; I was in prison and you came to Me.' [37] "Then the righteous will answer Him, saying, 'Lord, when did we see You hungry and feed *You,* or thirsty and give *You* drink? [38] When did we see You a stranger and take *You* in, or naked and clothe *You?* [39] Or when did we see You sick, or in prison, and come to You?' [40] And the King will answer and say to them, 'Assuredly, I say to you, inasmuch as you did *it* to one of the least of these My brethren, you did *it* to Me.' [41] "Then He will also say to those on the left hand, 'Depart from Me, you cursed, into the everlasting fire prepared for the devil and his angels: [42] for I was hungry and you gave Me no food; I was thirsty and you gave Me no drink; [43] I was a stranger and you did not take Me in, naked and you did not clothe Me, sick and in prison and you did not visit Me.' [44] "Then they also will answer Him, saying, 'Lord, when did we see You hungry or thirsty or a stranger or naked or sick or in prison, and did not minister to You?' [45] Then He will answer them, saying, 'Assuredly, I say to you, inasmuch as you did not do *it* to one of the least of these, you did not do *it* to Me.' [46] And these will go away into everlasting punishment, but the righteous into eternal life."

The world judges a faith by those who profess to be faithful! Faith demands works. The greater the faith, the greater the works, the greater the impact on the world. Yes, we are saved by grace. But there is the rest of that eternal truth: Because we are saved by His grace, we must be about His works.

A Christian life devoid of works is a disobedient and an unfruitful life. It is a withered branch unworthy of the True Vine. In fact, it gives rise to questions about the validity of the profession of faith. It is fit only to be cut off and cast aside. Strong words, especially in this day of "easy believism"? Perhaps, but, they were spoken by our Savior and our Lord (John 15:1-6).

The faith set forth in John 3:16 is not the modern "easy believism." It is not some passive, one-way gimmie-gimmie proposition. The faith in John 3:16 is a living, working faith (Gal. 5:6, 13-14; Heb. 13:20-21). It is a passionate state of heart and mind in the new man and the new woman who would turn the world right-side up for Christ.

A fruitless faith produces no works. It has no impact. It moves no mountains, generates no witness, contains no challenge, and obtains no victories. It lends aid and support to those who boast that "God is dead – or irrelevant."

The need for Christian works is great – and getting greater. It is needed in every area of life – in private and public squares, in the academies and in the pulpits and body of Christ's church...yes, especially in Christ's church!

If we fail in our obedience to the Lord God, if we fail to be about His work in all fields and all dimensions and tasks, Caesar will become even more powerful – indeed, all powerful and all-consuming. Thus will these generations raise up a god that brooks no competition, permits no diversity, acknowledges no personal liberty, permits no other authority – allows no other faith but Caesar's. We, as a nation (and indeed, as a world), now enter a system-shaking, society shattering, family-busting age – a time of tremendous change – an age of computers, robots, artificial intelligence, geopolitical strife, and global dictators. The stresses and the strains will be heightened by the magnitude of the changes and the speeds of events caused by the compression of time.

It is not only coming that we must choose who we will serve (have we not already made that choice!). It is more that we and our children must decide whether Christians will be leaders or slaves; whether we will be molders of, or molded by, the super state. Those decisions will be affected, in large measure, by whether we put our faith into works – everyday works:

- In the church and in the community

- Christian works of compassion and love

- Works of service to God and man

- Works of statecraft based on Biblical principle

- Works of education and communications in God's Word

- Works in all areas and in all things, for, is He not to have such preeminence?

Or shall we sleep in some misdirected, self-centered assurance that because we are saved by grace we can be above the fray while the church is manacled, the state is subverted, our treasury is stolen, and millions are aborted, or starved, or medically expended as useless and expensive aging relics?

Let it be said again and again. The followers of Christ are called to be leaders of men and nations! In 1843, Alexis deTocqueville wrote that "in no other country in the world does Christianity have as much influence as it has in the United States." Faith – and the power of faith. Faith and the works of faith. What would deTocqueville write about the Christians in this nation now?

THE WORDS OF FAITH

> **Romans 10:10** (NKJV) [10] For with the heart one believes unto righteousness, and with the mouth confession is made unto salvation.

There is a direct connection between faith in one's heart and the confession of one's mouth. If someone said he was a Christian and yet continually expressed doubt that he would go to heaven if he died, would that person have genuine faith in his heart?

It is a spiritual fact that the words of our mouths do express what is in our hearts (Matt. 12:34; 2 Cor. 4:13). The Greek word that is translated *"confess"* in Romans 10:10 literally means *"to say the same thing as, to agree with."* Therefore, when Christians confess their faith in God's Word, they are saying the same thing that God has said. From their hearts they are agreeing with and believing the Word of God. The words of our mouth do not create anything (only God does that), but our words do reveal the faith or unbelief that is in our hearts.

One of the most powerful phrases in the New Testament is *"the just shall live by faith."* This phrase is a quotation of Habakkuk 2:4, and it is found in three places in the New Testament: Romans 1:17; Galatians 3:11; Hebrews 10:38. We are saved by faith. We do not earn salvation, but we receive it by faith. We receive salvation by believing. But, exactly what do we believe to be saved?

> **1 Corinthians 15:1-4** (NKJV) [1] Moreover, brethren, I declare to you the gospel which I preached to you, which also you received and in which you stand, [2] by which also you are saved, if you hold fast that word which I preached to you—unless you believed in vain. [3] For I delivered to you first of all that which I also received: that Christ died for our sins according to the Scriptures, [4] and that He was buried, and that He rose again the third day according to the Scriptures,

Paul says we must believe:

1. Jesus died for our sins.

2. He was buried.

3. He rose again the third day.

4. What Jesus did fulfilled the Scriptures.

These facts necessarily imply a number of other facts:

1. We are lost, helpless sinners in need of a Savior.

2. Jesus was God and able to pay the penalty for our sins.

3. Jesus was sinless and able to rise from the dead.

4. The Scriptures are the Word of God.

However, merely "believing" these truths is not enough by itself:

> **James 2:19** (NKJV) [19] You believe that there is one God. You do well. Even the demons believe—and tremble!

We must also respond to Jesus:

John 6:37 (NKJV) [37] All that the Father gives Me will come to Me, and the one who comes to Me I will by no means cast out.

John 4:14 (NKJV) [14] but whoever drinks of the water that I shall give him will never thirst. But the water that I shall give him will become in him a fountain of water springing up into everlasting life."

Revelation 3:20 (NKJV) [20] Behold, I stand at the door and knock. If anyone hears My voice and opens the door, I will come in to him and dine with him, and he with Me.

In addition to believing the truths of the Gospel, we must also receive salvation. We must believe and receive:

John 1:12-13 (NKJV) [12] But as many as received Him, to them He gave the right to become children of God, to those who believe in His name: [13] who were born, not of blood, nor of the will of the flesh, nor of the will of man, but of God.

Romans 10:9 (NKJV) [9] that if you confess with your mouth the Lord Jesus and believe in your heart that God has raised Him from the dead, you will be saved.

To confess "Jesus is Lord" with your mouth means you surrender to Him as your Lord and God. It means to receive Him as your personal Lord and Savior. It means to turn from your own way and give your life to Jesus. It is at this point that you are "born again" and saved:

John 3:3 (NKJV) [3] Jesus answered and said to him, "Most assuredly, I say to you, unless one is born again, he cannot see the kingdom of God."

WE ARE SAVED BY FAITH ALONE

To be saved it is necessary to respond to Jesus and to receive His gift. Yet, that action of responding is not an act that merits salvation; it is merely a receiving of His free gift. We are saved by faith and not by works (though works are an important part of the expression of our Christianity as we have discussed before):

> **Titus 3:5** (NKJV) [5] not by works of righteousness which we have done, but according to His mercy He saved us, through the washing of regeneration and renewing of the Holy Spirit,

We do not earn salvation in any sense. Even the faith by which we appropriate God's gift of salvation is itself a gift from God:

> **Ephesians 2:8-9** (NKJV) [8] For by grace you have been saved through faith, and that not of yourselves; *it is* the gift of God, [9] not of works, lest anyone should boast.

> **Acts 18:27** (NKJV) [27] And when he desired to cross to Achaia, the brethren wrote, exhorting the disciples to receive him; and when he arrived, he greatly helped those who had believed through grace;

> **Philippians 1:29** (NKJV) [29] For to you it has been granted on behalf of Christ, not only to believe in Him, but also to suffer for His sake,

Faith is a gift from the Father (Rom. 12:3), from the Son of God (Heb. 12:2), and from the Holy Spirit (Gal. 5:22). There is nothing we can do that in any way makes us deserve or earn God's salvation. Salvation is an entirely free gift received by faith (Rom. 4:4-5).

Paul says we either deserve salvation because of our own good works or we receive it as a free undeserved gift; it cannot be both (Rom. 3:27-28). Because all men have sinned, it is impossible for anyone to deserve eternal life. So, to approach God on the basis of your works and to try to receive eternal life as if it were something you deserve for your righteous life is to guarantee that you will not receive it. Look at the example of Israel:

> **Romans 9:31-32** (NKJV) [31] but Israel, pursuing the law of righteousness, has not attained to the law of righteousness. [32] Why? Because *they did* not *seek it* by faith, but as it were, by the works of the law. For they stumbled at that stumbling stone.

As long as a man tries to earn salvation by his own works, he cannot experience the salvation of God that is received as a free gift by faith alone.

> **Romans 6:23** (NKJV) [23] For the wages of sin *is* death, but the gift of God *is* eternal life in Christ Jesus our Lord.

"Wages" are what we earn; "wages" are what we deserve. A "gift" is what we have not earned; a "gift" is what we do not deserve. Because all men have sinned, the only thing anyone deserves from God is death, but because of His love, God provided salvation to us as a gift through Jesus' death on the cross. Because it is a gift, we do not deserve it; we have not earned it. We receive salvation as a free, unmerited gift from God; and we receive it by faith. As we surrender our lives to the lordship of Jesus Christ, we believe that God has saved us through Jesus' death on the cross.

FAITH AND REPENTANCE

Many times in the Scriptures, faith and repentance are spoken of side by side.

By Jesus:

> **Mark 1:14-15** (NKJV) [14] Now after John was put in prison, Jesus

came to Galilee, preaching the gospel of the kingdom of God, [15] and saying, "The time is fulfilled, and the kingdom of God is at hand. Repent, and believe in the gospel."

By Paul:

> **Acts 20:21** (NKJV) [21] testifying to Jews, and also to Greeks, repentance toward God and faith toward our Lord Jesus Christ.

At the point that a man or woman receives salvation, both repentance and faith are present. The man or woman looks at the sin of their life, in repentance, and then turns from his or her own way, in faith, to God's provision of the cross.

In salvation, we turn from the old life with repentance, and we turn to the Lord Jesus with faith.

> **1 Thessalonians 1:9** (NKJV) [9] For they themselves declare concerning us what manner of entry we had to you, and how you turned to God from idols to serve the living and true God,

From this, we see that the true preaching of repentance must always be accompanied by the positive message of faith in God's provision. On the other hand, the true Biblical message of faith must always be accompanied by repentance. Without faith, repentance turns into remorse and condemnation and is fruitless; without repentance, faith has no ground for receiving anything from a Holy God.

THE GROWTH OF FAITH

In Galatians 5, Paul speaks of the fruit of the Spirit, and one of the fruits he mentions is faith:

> **Galatians 5:22-23** (NKJV) [22] But the fruit of the Spirit is love, joy,

peace, longsuffering, kindness, goodness, faithfulness, [23] gentleness, self-control. Against such there is no law.

One of the characteristics of a fruit is that it grows over a period of time. That is true of faith.

> **2 Thessalonians 1:3** (NKJV) [3] We are bound to thank God always for you, brethren, as it is fitting, because your faith grows exceedingly, and the love of every one of you all abounds toward each other,

In the Scriptures, faith is spoken of as having varying degrees. For example:

"Little faith"

> **Matthew 8:26** (NKJV) [26] But He said to them, "Why are you fearful, O you of little faith?" Then He arose and rebuked the winds and the sea, and there was a great calm.

"Weak faith"

> **Romans 14:1** (NKJV) [1] Receive one who is weak in the faith, *but* not to disputes over doubtful things.

"Useless faith"

> **James 2:20** (NKJV) [20] But do you want to know, O foolish man, that faith without works is dead?

"Great faith"

> **Luke 7:9** (NKJV) [9] When Jesus heard these things, He marveled at him, and turned around and said to the crowd that followed Him, "I say to you, I have not found such great faith, not even in Israel!"

"Full of faith"

Acts 6:8 (NKJV) [8] And Stephen, full of faith and power, did great wonders and signs among the people.

"Rich in faith"

> **James 2:5** (NKJV) [5] Listen, my beloved brethren: Has God not chosen the poor of this world *to be* rich in faith and heirs of the kingdom which He promised to those who love Him?

In Romans 12, Paul speaks of the ***"measure of faith"*** that God has given every Christian:

> **Romans 12:3** (NKJV) [3] For I say, through the grace given to me, to everyone who is among you, not to think *of himself* more highly than he ought to think, but to think soberly, as God has dealt to each one a measure of faith.

So we see that faith can be great or little. How can we then grow in our faith and be strong before God? The answer is found in Romans 10:

> **Romans 10:17** (NKJV) [17] So then faith *comes* by hearing, and hearing by the word of God.

We can see the divine order from this verse: the Word of God comes first, then "hearing," and then faith. In other words, the Word of God is first preached or taught. Then the listener attends to that word with a desire to receive and obey it (i.e., he "hears" it). Finally, faith is produced in his heart.

<u>There are three important things we can learn from this progression.</u>

Firstly, it must be the Word of God that is heard. The word of human tradition will not produce faith. Errors and heresy will not produce faith. It must be the Word of God.

Jesus told the religious leaders of His day that the Word of God, which should have been powerful in their lives, had been made ineffective by their human traditions:

> **Matthew 15:6** (NKJV) [6] then he need not honor his father or mother.' Thus you have made the commandment of God of no effect by your tradition.

Secondly, there must be "hearing." The Word of God falling upon disinterested or disobedient ears will not produce faith. No matter how many books you read, tapes you hear, sermons you listen to, or meetings you attend, if you do not listen to the Word of God with a heart that is willing to receive and obey, faith will never grow in your heart. It will never happen.

This is one reason why so many Christians today are weak in faith. They spend so little time in the Word – and what time they do spend is usually hurried and haphazard – that faith never had the chance to grow. Furthermore, the word that is preached today is often so diluted with man's opinions, theories and misconceptions, that even if you studied it night and day it still would produce little faith.

Thirdly, when the Word is "heard" by an attentive and sincere heart, faith will come. As you diligently spend time in the Word of God and listen to anointed scriptural teaching, you will grow stronger in your faith. It will work. Your faith will grow.

Paul commended the Thessalonian Christians for their "faith (that was) growing more and more" (2 Thessalonians 1:3). This is because these believers had "received the word" and had diligently obeyed it (1 Thessalonians 1:6-10).

For your faith to grow continually, you must spend daily time in the Word, as well as time in the congregation of the saints listening to the public preaching and teaching of the Word of God.

But rest assured that your labors will not be in vain. The Word of God is alive and powerful, and as you do "hear" the Word with an attentive and obedient heart, faith will come.

SUMMARY

Faith in God develops gradually in our lives as we mature in Christ and

yield to His supremacy. It is impossible to please God apart from having faith. It is faith that saves, keeps, and matures us.

We grow in faith as we increase in knowledge of the Word of God and as we respond in obedience to the Holy Spirit's leading. Moving in faith as God directs and then seeing the results of that faith spur us on to ever greater faith.

Without faith, there is a tendency to try to please God through works, as futile as that is. But true faith always leads us to God and His promises. It gives assurance for the present and hope for the future. It brings us to increasingly higher realms of relationship with God. It is how we are called to live: "The righteous will live by faith." (Rom. 1:17).

CHAPTER 7

THE DOCTRINE OF BAPTISMS

In Hebrews 6, the next foundational doctrine that is mentioned is "instruction about baptisms." Please notice that "baptism" is plural. There is more than one kind of baptism mentioned in the New Testament. There are four baptisms spoken of in the New Testament:

1. The baptism of John (Matt. 3:11)

2. The Lord's baptism of suffering (Luke 12:50)

3. Christian baptism (Acts 2:38)

4. Baptism of the Holy Spirit (Acts 11:16)

Before we look at each of these, let us first examine the meaning of the term "baptism" itself.

THE MEANING OF "BAPTISM"

The word Baptism is not initially an English word, but rather an Anglicized Greek word. The Greek verb that is translated "baptism" in the New Testament is *baptizo* which means to put into or under water (or other penetrable substance so as to entirely immerse or submerse.) It can also mean to cleanse by dipping or submerging, or to wash. Metaphorically it can mean to overwhelm (e.g. Isaiah 21:4). This word is always translated "baptize" in the New Testament except in a couple of places:

> **Mark 7:4** (NKJV) [4] When they come from the marketplace, they do not eat unless they wash. And there are many other things which they have received and hold, *like* the washing of cups,

pitchers, copper vessels, and couches.

Luke 11:38 (NKJV) [38] When the Pharisee saw *it,* he marveled that He had not first washed before dinner.

Furthermore, the word is used several times in the Greek Septuagint version of the Old Testament. Its usage in 2 Kings 5:14 gives us insight into the meaning of the word. The English version reads:

> *So he went down and **dipped** himself in the Jordan seven times, as the man of God had told him, and his flesh was restored and became clean like that of a young boy (2 Kings 5:14).*

The noun ***baptisma*** means immersion or submersion. The word is used in the following Scripture:

> *And they observed many other traditions, such as the **washing** (lit. "baptisms") of cups, pitchers and kettles (Mark 7:4).*

The most basic root of *baptizo* is the verb *bapto*, which means to dip, immerse or cover wholly with fluid. This verb is used in several New Testament verses:

> *So he called to him, "Father Abraham, have pity on me and send Lazarus to **dip** the tip of his finger in water and cool my tongue, because I am in agony in this fire" (Luke 16:24).*

> *Jesus answered, "It is the one to whom I give this piece of bread when I have **dipped** it in the dish"... (John 13:26).*

> *He is dressed in a robe **dipped** in blood... (Rev. 19:13).*

In all of these passages the key idea behind "baptism" is an immersion or dipping; something is dipped into a fluid and then taken out again.

This is confirmed by Classical and Apocryphal usage of the word:

1. In the fifth or fourth century B.C. *baptizo* was used by Plato of a young man being "overwhelmed" by clever philosophical arguments.

2. In the writings of Hippocrates (fourth century B.C.), *baptizo* was used of people being "submerged" in water and of sponges being "dipped" in water.

3. Between 100 B.C. and A.D. 100, *baptizo* was used by Strabo to describe people who could not swim being "submerged" beneath the surface of the water.

4. In the first century, *baptizo* was used metaphorically by Josephus to describe both a man "plunging" a sword into his own neck and Jerusalem being "overwhelmed" or "plunged" into destruction by internal strife.

5. In the first or second century, *baptizo* was used twice by Plutarach to describe either the body of a person or the figure of an idol being "immersed" in the sea.

6. In the Apocryphal book of Judith (12:7), when Judith went out each night and "bathed" at the spring, the word *baptizo* was used.

So, the meaning of baptism is clearly established as an immersion or dipping in fluid. Furthermore, this immersion is usually temporary.

Now, we will examine the four baptisms of the New Testament.

JOHN'S BAPTISM (MARK 1:4)

John was a distinctive person.

- He was the son of Zacharias and Elizabeth (Luke 1:5, 13).

- He was the greatest of the prophets (Luke 7:28).

- He was sent to introduce Jesus to Israel (John 1:31; Matt. 3:3; Luke 1:76-77).

The significance of John's Baptism

- He was divinely sent to baptize (John 1:33).

- His ministry marked the beginning of a new age (Luke 16:16).

- His ministry marked a new order of divine requirement (Luke 3:2-3).

- It was "the counsel (purpose, will) of God" for that time (Luke 7:30).

- Those who were baptized, "justified God" (declaring God to be right in His demands) (Luke 7:29).

- John's baptism was superseded by Christian baptism (Acts 19:4-5).

That the baptism of John was different from Christian water baptism is evident by Paul's response to the believers in Ephesus who had experienced only John's baptism (Acts 19:4-5). This signifies that Paul considered John's baptism as quite distinct from Christian baptism. Furthermore, he obviously did not consider John's baptism sufficient for a believer since he baptized these believers again in the name of Jesus.

John's baptism was a baptism of repentance (Acts 19:4). This was a preparatory ministry to make the people ready to receive the coming Messiah. Those who received John's baptism confessed their sins and enjoyed a real experience of repentance and forgiveness of sins, and their lives were changed. [In much the same way, the Old Testament saints had their sins truly forgiven when they offered animal sacrifices in faith and obedience. Their sins were forgiven, ultimately, only by Jesus' blood. Yet, as they obeyed the light they had in repentance and faith, they were saved (cf. Rom. 3:25-26).] However, John's baptism was only the precursor of the ministry of the Messiah where the people would truly receive the fullness of the abiding, inward peace through the grace of God (Rom. 5:1).

By itself, John's baptism could never give the people ultimate righteousness or peace. Rather, it was to prepare the people to receive and respond to the Messiah when He came. That was the meaning of his baptism.

John's baptism was a baptism of repentance, but Jesus had never sinned and did not need to be baptized. John himself recognized this (Matt 3:14). However Jesus answered:

> ..."Let it be so now; it is proper for us to do this to fulfill all righteousness." Then John consented (Matt. 3:15).

Jesus was not baptized by John as the outward evidence that He had repented of His sins. Jesus was baptized to "fulfill all righteousness." Jesus was setting an example or pattern of obedience for His disciples to follow. He was showing us by example what He expects us to do. Jesus obeyed His Father in the outward act of baptism even though He was sinless. Even so, we who have been saved by His death on the cross should follow Him in the act of baptism "to fulfill all righteousness." By faith in Jesus we become righteous, and baptism is an outward sign of identification with Him in His death. So, while John's baptism was a baptism of repentance, Christian baptism following Jesus' example will indeed "fulfill all righteousness." It will complete by an outward act of obedience the inward righteousness which the believer already enjoys by faith in his heart.

Furthermore, Jesus' baptism was also an outward act of consecration to death for the sins of the world. Baptism is a symbol of death and Jesus' baptism was a type of His future death on the cross when He accepted the place of the sinner and bore his punishment. Jesus did not need to be baptized any more than He deserved to die. But, just as His death on the cross was in substitution for the sins of others, so His baptism in water was a consecration to that substitutionary act. In this way, too, Jesus' baptism by John "fulfilled all righteousness."

THE BAPTISM OF SUFFERING (MARK 10:38)

Jesus here referred to His own sufferings and death on the cross figuratively as a "baptism." He also indicated that His disciples would be called to experience this same immersion in suffering and death (Mark 10:39).

This union of Christ and His disciples in suffering is also spoken of by Paul (Rom. 8:17; 2 Tim. 2:12). Suffering is part of the normal Christian life. We won't expound further on this topic at this time, but it is of critical importance to understand as part of our Christian experience and growth. An entire chapter will be devoted to this subject.

CHRISTIAN WATER BAPTISM

To be baptized in water as a Christian was not a suggestion by Jesus; it was His commandment:

> **Matthew 28:19** (NKJV) [19] Go therefore and make disciples of all the nations, baptizing them in the name of the Father and of the Son and of the Holy Spirit,

> **Mark 16:16** (NKJV) [16] He who believes and is baptized will be saved; but he who does not believe will be condemned.

Acts 10:48 (NKJV) [48] And he commanded them to be baptized in the name of the Lord. Then they asked him to stay a few days.

We are saved by faith alone without works of any kind, but a faith that saves will always produce obedience to God. Therefore, we must understand and practice Christian water baptism.

The Conditions for Baptism

The conditions to receive Christian water baptism are as follows:

1. Hearing and heeding the Word (Acts 2:41; 16:14-15; 19:5).

2. Conviction (Acts 2:37).

3. Repentance (Acts 2:38).

4. Faith (Mark 16:16; Acts 8:12, 36-37; 16:31-33).

5. Obedience (Acts 9:6).

When a person has believed the Gospel and turned from his sins, then he is eligible to be baptized in water.

How Soon Should a New Believer Be Baptized?

It is clear from the Book of Acts that a new believer should be baptized **without delay**.

1. Peter's preaching on the Day of Pentecost (Acts 2:38) and the people's response (Acts 2:41).

2. Philip's ministry in Samaria (Acts 8:12).

3. Philip's ministry to the eunuch from Ethiopia (Acts 8:36-38).

4. Saul's salvation experience (Acts 9:17-18; cf. 22:16).

5. The household of Cornelius (Acts 10:44-48).

6. The household of Lydia (Acts 16:14-15).

7. The household of the jailer at Philippi (Acts 16:31-33).

8. Crispus and the Corinthians (Acts 18:8).

9. The believers at Ephesus (Acts 19:5).

We have just looked at every single instance of water baptism recorded in the Book of Acts! What did we find? Without exception, salvation is followed as soon as possible by water baptism. The longest period of time between salvation and water baptism in the Book of Acts was three days in the case of Saul (Acts 9:9).

The Nature of Water Baptism

1. New Testament water baptism is **by full immersion**.

   - See previous word study on *baptizo* and *bapto*. The word itself means immersion.

   - John the Baptist baptized in a certain place near Salim "because there was plenty of water" (John 3:23).

   - When Jesus was baptized in Matthew 3:16 it was said that He "went up out of the water." The language used speaks of a full immersion.

   - Concerning Philip and the eunuch went down into the water and Philip baptized him" (Acts 8:38). The next verse says, "when they came up out of the water..." (Acts 8:39). Again, the language used speaks of a full immersion.

   - In Romans 6, Paul speaks of baptism as being an outward picture of our union with Jesus in His death, burial, and resurrection (Rom. 6:4).

To be "buried...through baptism" obviously implies full immersion (see also Col. 2:12).

- The passing of the Israelites through the Red Sea was a type of Christian water baptism (1 Cor. 10:1-2); this event clearly signifies full immersion.

- Noah's ark was said by Peter to symbolize water baptism in that both are types of our salvation in Christ (1 Pet. 3:20-21). This parallel again indicates full immersion.

- Other Typological references to water baptism:

  o The Red Sea Crossing (Ex. 12-14). Three elements: The blood of the Passover Lamb; the water of the Red Sea and the cloud of the Lord's presence.

  o Washing and sprinkling of Israel at the giving of the Law (Exodus 19:10-11; Heb. 9:19-20).

  o The laver in the Tabernacle courtyard (Heb. 9:8-9). The laver was a place of self-examination (Exodus 30:17-21; 40:7). No priest could enter the Holy Place without cleansing and changing his garments.

  o Washing of priests at their consecration (Ex. 29:1-7; compare 1 John 2:20, 27 with John 14:16-17, 26).

  o Washing of animal sacrifices (Lev. 1;1-13; 1 Kings 18:33-39).

  o Washing and sprinkling of lepers who were healed (Lev. 14).

  o Washing of the ceremonially unclean (Num. 19).

  o Washing of spoils of war and warriors' clothing (Num. 31:1-18, 21-24).

- o Noah's flood (1 Peter 3:20-24).

- o Circumcision.

- A close look at some of these types indicates the role of baptism as a cleansing from sin.

  - o Before the priest could enter the Tabernacle he had to wash at the laver; otherwise God would strike him dead (Ex. 30:20).

  - o A ceremonially unclean person had to wash with water before he could become clean (Lev. 15; 17:15-16; Num. 19; compare Ezekiel 36:25).

    - ▪ This was "the water of separation...a purification for sin" (Num. 19:9) or the "water of cleansing...for purification from sin" (NIV).

    - ▪ If the unclean person refused to wash in this manner, he continued to bear his iniquity (Lev. 17:16; Num. 19:13, 20).

- A close look at some of these types shows that blood was applied by means of water.

  - o This indicates that in water baptism, the blood of Christ is applied for remission of sins.

  - o After the giving of the Law at Mt. Sinai, Moses mixed blood and water and sprinkled it on the people (Heb. 9:19).

  - o When cleansing the ex-leper, the priest mixed a bird's blood and water and sprinkled it on the person (Lev. 14:1-7).

- In order to prepare the water of purification for an unclean person, the priest killed a red heifer and burned it as a sacrifice, with much of its blood still in it (Num. 19:1-5).

- The ashes became equivalent to blood as a purifying agent (Heb. 9:13) and were mixed with water to make the water of purification (Num. 19:9).

- In all these cases, water was the means by which the atoning blood was applied.

2. New Testament water baptism is always of adults or children old enough to believe and repent, and it is **never of infants**. [i](for more in-depth information on this topic see *Excursus: Infant Baptism* from RLB message "*Dedication or Baptism of Infants*" given at Master Builder Christian Church – 3/14/2004 at the end of this book.)

- In the Bible, there is neither a command to baptize infants nor any example of infant baptism. Furthermore, infant baptism is expressly contradicted by the teaching of Scripture. The following are proofs of this:

    - If Jesus and His disciples had been in the habit of baptizing infants, then Jesus' disciples would not have forbidden the little children to come to Him (Matt. 19:13-14).

    - 1 Corinthians 7:14 refutes infant baptism since Paul would certainly have referred to the baptism of children as a proof of their consecration to the Lord if infant baptism had been practiced.

    - Conscious faith and repentance are the scriptural prerequisites for water baptism, and babies are incapable of both. Mark speaks of baptizing "believers" (Mark 16:16), and Matthew speaks of baptizing "disciples" (Matt. 28:19); infants are neither "believers" nor "disciples."

- o To practice infant baptism is not only unscriptural but is actually very dangerous because it leads logically to the further error of baptismal regeneration. It encourages the parents and the child as he grows up to believe the false notion that the outward act of sprinkling water on the baby's head had some actual saving efficacy associated with it. Therefore, the child will grow up with a false sense of confidence and security that he is right with God simply because of his baptism at infancy.

3. Jesus died only once (Heb. 10:10-14; 1 Pet. 3:18). Since we are baptized into union with His death, we are to be immersed only once (and not three times as some practice).

4. New Testament water baptism is performed in Jesus' name. We shall look at every water baptism in the Book of Acts where a name is given:

   a. **Acts 2:38** (NKJV) [38] Then Peter said to them, "Repent, and let every one of you be baptized in the name of Jesus Christ for the remission of sins; and you shall receive the gift of the Holy Spirit.

   b. **Acts 8:16** (NKJV) [16] For as yet He had fallen upon none of them. They had only been baptized in the name of the Lord Jesus.

   c. **Acts 10:48** (NKJV) [48] And he commanded them to be baptized in the name of the Lord. Then they asked him to stay a few days.

d. **Acts 19:5** (NKJV) [5] When they heard *this,* they were baptized in the name of the Lord Jesus.

e. **Acts 22:16** (NKJV) [16] And now why are you waiting? Arise and be baptized, and wash away your sins, calling on the name of the Lord.'

Obviously the clear evidence is that New Testament water baptism should be done in the name of Jesus. Many churches, however, follow Matthew 28:19 for their baptismal 'formula."

How do we reconcile this? Jesus told His disciples to baptize "in the name of the Father and of the Son and of the Holy Spirit"; yet, the same disciples who heard that command went out and obeyed it **by** baptizing new believers in the name of the Lord Jesus. There is not a single example anywhere in the New Testament of anyone ever being baptized "in the name of the Father and of the Son and of the Holy Spirit." Furthermore, there is additional compelling evidence that we should use the name of Jesus for water baptism.

The name of Jesus is exalted, glorified and used throughout the New Testament. Where in the New Testament does anyone ever heal the sick, cast out a demon, raise the dead, or receive a prayer request from God in the name of the Father and of the Son and of the Holy Spirit? On the contrary, it is always, without exception, done in the name of Jesus (Mark 16:17-18; Luke 10:17; 24:47; John 14:13, 26; 15:16; 16:23, 26; Acts 3:6; 4:12, 30; Eph. 5:20; Jam. 5:14).

In Colossians 3:17, Paul says, "whatever you do, whether in word or deed, do it all in the name of the Lord Jesus..." Certainly this would include water baptism.

The same apostles who received the commission of Matthew 28:19 obeyed Jesus by baptizing in the name of Jesus. They did not make a mistake. The reconciliation is simple.

For in him dwelleth all the fullness of the Godhead bodily (Col. 2:9, KJV).

"He is the exact likeness of the unseen God, the visible representation of the invisible...for it hath pleased (the Father) that all the divine fullness –the sum total the divine perfection, powers, and attributes –should dwell, in Him permanently" (Col. 1:15, 19 Amplified).

"For it is in Christ that the fullness of God's nature dwells embodied" (Col. 2:9 Weymouth).

The name of God was considered to be too holy to be uttered by the people of God in the Old Testament. We know this translated as Jehovah. However, the Israelites substituted for it, the word Lord (*Adonai*). The American Standard Version translated the "Incommunicable name" Jehovah, instead of following the practice of using "Lord."

God has many descriptive titles, but there is no question as to His name:

Exodus 6:2-3 (Amplified) "And God said to Moses, I am the Lord, I appeared to Abraham, to Isaac, and to Jacob, as God Almighty [*El Shaddai*], but by My name the Lord [*Yahweh*] [the redemptive name of God] – I did not make Myself known to them [in acts and great miracles]."

Psalm 83:18 (NKJV) [18] That they may know that You, whose name alone *is* the LORD, *Are* the Most High over all the earth.

Isaiah 47:4 (ASV) [4] Our Redeemer, Jehovah of hosts is his name, the Holy One of Israel.

We can see the revelation of God in Christ through the following scriptural verses:

1 Timothy 3:16 (NKJV) [16] And without controversy great is the mystery of godliness: God was manifested in the flesh, Justified in the Spirit, Seen by angels, Preached among the Gentiles, Believed on in the world, Received up in glory.

The writer of Hebrews tells us that the God of the Old Testament was the God who:

Hebrews 1:1-4 (NKJV) [1] God, who at various times and in various ways spoke in time past to the fathers by the prophets, [2] has in these last days spoken to us by *His* Son, whom He has appointed heir of all things, through whom also He made the worlds; [3] who being the brightness of *His* glory and the express image of His person, and upholding all things by the word of His power, when He had by Himself purged our sins, sat down at the right hand of the Majesty on high, [4] having become so much better than the angels, as He has by inheritance obtained a more excellent name than they.

The name "Lord" which the Old Testament used for Jehovah was now given to Jesus Christ. This indicates that God was in Christ

2 Corinthians 5:19 (NKJV) [19] that is, that God was in Christ reconciling the world to Himself, not imputing their trespasses to them, and has committed to us the word of reconciliation.

Matthew 1:21 (NKJV) [21] And she will bring forth a Son, and you shall call His name JESUS, for He will save His people from their sins."

Matthew 1:23 (NKJV) [23] *"Behold, the virgin shall be with child, and bear a Son, and they shall call His name Immanuel,"* which is translated, "God with us."

Acts 2:36 (NKJV) [36] "Therefore let all the house of Israel know assuredly that God has made this Jesus, whom you crucified, both Lord and Christ."

The Spirit of Truth, according to the Scriptures, revealed to the apostles and disciples, and to the church, the fact that the name of the Father and of the Son and of the Holy Spirit, is the name of the Lord.

"Jesus" is the name of God, and in Jesus dwells all the fullness of the triune Godhead bodily. So, to baptize in the name of Jesus is to obey the command to baptize in the name of the Godhead. To baptize into Jesus is to baptize into the triune God because the triune God dwells fully in Him. God is one, and all of God is in the Lord Jesus Christ. "Jesus" is the name of God.

Water baptism, like everything else in the New Testament, is always in the name of Jesus. "Jesus" is the name of God. "Father," "Son" and "Holy Spirit" are not names, but titles. "Father" is not a name, but a title. If you were to ask a child of reasonable age, "What is your father's name?" surely he would not answer "father." Likewise, "Son" is not a name, but a title. Proverbs 30:4, says "...What is his name, and the name of his son? Tell me if you know!" Jesus commanded us to baptize in the name (singular) of God. "Jesus" is the name by which God has revealed Himself on this earth (Acts 4:12; Heb. 1:2). "Jesus" is the name of God.

In Paul's teaching about water baptism, he always says we were baptized into Jesus; he never once says our baptism was into the Father, Son and Holy Spirit:

> **Romans 6:3** (NKJV) [3] Or do you not know that as many of us as were baptized into Christ Jesus were baptized into His death?

> **Galatians 3:27** (NKJV) [27] For as many of you as were baptized into Christ have put on Christ.

> **Colossians 2:12** (NKJV) [12] buried with Him in baptism, in which you also were raised with *Him* through faith in the working of God, who raised Him from the dead.

Baptism is a picture of our union with Jesus in His death and resurrection. Jesus is the One who died for us. The Father and the Holy Spirit never died! Jesus is the One who died and then was raised, yet, because the fullness of the Godhead dwells in Christ, when we are baptized in the name of Jesus, we are baptized in the triune God because God is one and Jesus is God. "Jesus" is the name of God.

One of Paul's most characteristic expressions is "en Christo" (in Christ). Paul says the believer is "in Christ." However, because God is one and Jesus is God, we are in the fullness of the triune Godhead when we are in Christ.

All the blessings of redemption are "in Christ", so, water baptism, an outward witness of the entrance of the believer into union with the Son of God, must also be into "the name of Jesus." In the Bible, the name of God and God Himself are often equated. When you are baptized into the "name of the Lord Jesus," you are baptized into union with Jesus Christ, and you are made to be "in Christ" and partakers of the benefits of redemption.

The simplest proof of this truth is that every baptism in the Book of Acts, without exception, is performed "in the name of Jesus."

While recognizing that full immersion in the name of Jesus is the New Testament mode, the spirit of baptism and commitment to the Lord Jesus are of more importance than the exact form. In other words, the most important thing is that the new believer is baptized in water. The mode of baptism should not become an issue of division.

The Meaning of Water Baptism

Water baptism is an outward act depicting what has already happened inside the heart and life of the new believer. Water baptism graphically depicts several spiritual realities.

1. Union with Jesus

a. Baptism signifies that we are united with Jesus in His death and burial (Col. 2:12).

When you were born again, your "old man" died. Your old life came to an end. All connection with sin and self was potentially severed. That will become a spiritual reality in your life as you embrace it by faith and walk in it.

We were united with Jesus in His death; we died to sin, self and the power of the world:

> **Romans 6:6-7** (NKJV) [6] knowing this, that our old man was crucified with *Him,* that the body of sin might be done away with, that we should no longer be slaves of sin. [7] For he who has died has been freed from sin.

> **Galatians 6:14** (NKJV) [14] But God forbid that I should boast except in the cross of our Lord Jesus Christ, by whom the world has been crucified to me, and I to the world.

In our union with Jesus, we also died to the law:

> **Galatians 2:19** (NKJV) [19] For I through the law died to the law that I might live to God.

Sin, self, the world and the law all have as much power over you as they do over a dead body! That is what happened when you were saved, and water baptism graphically depicts it: you died with Christ. The old man is now dead; he has no power or strength unless you give it to him. Victory is yours, but you must choose to walk in it:

> **Romans 6:11** (NKJV) [11] Likewise you also, reckon yourselves to be dead indeed to sin, but alive to God in Christ Jesus our Lord.

> **Galatians 5:24-25** (NKJV) [24] And those *who are* Christ's have crucified the flesh with its passions and desires. [25] If we live in the Spirit, let us also walk in the Spirit.

b. Baptism signifies that we were united with Jesus in His resurrection.

Romans 6:4 (NKJV) [4] Therefore we were buried with Him through baptism into death, that just as Christ was raised from the dead by the glory of the Father, even so we also should walk in newness of life.

Romans 6:11 (NKJV) [11] Likewise you also, reckon yourselves to be dead indeed to sin, but alive to God in Christ Jesus our Lord.

In union with Jesus' resurrection, we were made alive to God, to righteousness and to newness of life. Again, this is a spiritual reality in Christ. A new life in Christ – a life of victory and fellowship with Him – is ours if we will believe it and walk in it:

2 Corinthians 5:17 (NKJV) [17] Therefore, if anyone *is* in Christ, *he is* a new creation; old things have passed away; behold, all things have become new.

Romans 6:10-13 (NKJV) [10] For *the death* that He died, He died to sin once for all; but *the life* that He lives, He lives to God. [11] Likewise you also, reckon yourselves to be dead indeed to sin, but alive to God in Christ Jesus our Lord. [12] Therefore do not let sin reign in your mortal body, that you should obey it in its lusts. [13] And do not present your members *as* instruments of unrighteousness to sin, but present yourselves to God as being alive from the dead, and your members *as* instruments of righteousness to God.

Romans 6:17-18 (NKJV) [17] But God be thanked that *though* you were slaves of sin, yet you obeyed from the heart that form of doctrine to which you were delivered. [18] And having been set free from sin, you became slaves of righteousness.

When this truth of your union with Jesus in His death, burial and resurrection becomes a reality in your heart it will produce a radical outward change in your life. Our new life is life "after His image" and His image is an image of holiness, righteousness, truth, humility and godly character:

> **Galatians 3:27** (NKJV) [27] For as many of you as were baptized into Christ have put on Christ.

> **Colossians 3:9-10** (NKJV) [9] Do not lie to one another, since you have put off the old man with his deeds, [10] and have put on the new *man* who is renewed in knowledge according to the image of Him who created him,

> **Ephesians 4:22-24** (NKJV) [22] that you put off, concerning your former conduct, the old man which grows corrupt according to the deceitful lusts, [23] and be renewed in the spirit of your mind, [24] and that you put on the new man which was created according to God, in true righteousness and holiness.

When we were saved, we were united with Jesus in His death, and we died to sin, self and the world. Then, we were raised with Jesus into newness of life in God. This is the transforming reality of what it means to be a Christian, and it is all depicted by water baptism!

2. **Water baptism also signifies the washing away of our sins and the cleansing of our consciences which happened when we were saved:**

1 Peter 3:21 (NKJV) [21] There is also an antitype which now saves us—baptism (not the removal of the filth of the flesh, but the answer of a good conscience toward God), through the resurrection of Jesus Christ,

3. **Water baptism is also a public declaration of the new believer's faith in Christ.**

Mark 10:32-33 (NKJV) [32] Now they were on the road, going up to Jerusalem, and Jesus was going before them; and they were amazed. And as they followed they were afraid. Then He took the twelve aside again and began to tell them the things that would happen to Him: [33] "Behold, we are going up to Jerusalem, and the Son of Man will be betrayed to the chief priests and to the scribes; and they will condemn Him to death and deliver Him to the Gentiles;

Does Baptism Save?

Over the centuries it has been taught by some that baptism works a magical way to produce regeneration, and that it secures automatic forgiveness of all past sins and is essential to salvation. The Roman Catholic Church, for example, has taught:

Baptism may be accurately and appositely defined to be the sacrament of regeneration by water in the word. For by nature we are born from Adam children of wrath, but by baptism we are regenerated in Christ children of mercy. (*Council of Trident*, Pt. 2, Ch. 2, Ques. 5)

This means that unless someone has been baptized in water they can never be saved. Therefore, if a child dies before being baptized, he is automatically lost. To deal with this problem, the Roman Catholics have even gone so far as to invent a means of prenatal baptism.

In reply, we say the Bible teaches that water baptism is only an outward sign of what has already occurred within an individual; therefore, only those who have already repented and been born again should be baptized in water.

In Matthew 3:5-8, John commanded the Pharisees and Sadducees to bring forth fruits proving they had repented before he would baptize them. Many references in the Book of Acts show that people were always saved before they were baptized in water: Acts 2:41; 8:12-13, 35-38; 9:4-6, 17-18; 10:44-48 (certainly God would not have given the Holy Spirit to people who weren't even saved!); 16:14-15, 30-34; 18:8; 19:1-5.

The symbolic nature of water baptism is evident from Jesus' own baptism that could not possibly have been for the purpose of regeneration and cleansing from sin since Jesus was already pure and holy.

Furthermore, the Bible teaches that we are saved by faith alone, without any works of any kind:

> **Titus 3:5** (NKJV) [5] not by works of righteousness which we have done, but according to His mercy He saved us, through the washing of regeneration and renewing of the Holy Spirit,
>
> Cf. Romans 2:25-29; 3:28; 4:3-6; Galatians 2:16; 5:6; 6:15

Justification is by faith alone and can never be by any outward rite. The thief on the cross was saved by his faith alone (Luke 23:43) and was obviously never baptized.

In Romans 4, Paul teaches that Abraham was justified by his faith alone long before he was circumcised. Abraham's circumcision was simply a "sign" and a "seal" of the righteousness which he already had through his faith (verse 11). Paul wrote this to refute a particular Jewish error of his day which was that connection with Abraham by natural descent and by the bond of circumcision together with the observance of the law was sufficient to obtain the favor of God. Religious man has not changed, and the same error is taught today in a different form by those who trust that participation in an outward act is sufficient to save them (cf. Matthew 23:25-26).

Finally, 1 Peter 3:21 teaches that it is "not the removal of dirt from the body" in water that saves us. Rather, baptism is simply evidence of what has already happened in the heart of a person who has believed on Jesus and therefore has a good conscience toward God.

CHAPTER 8

THE BAPTISM OF THE HOLY SPIRIT

Speaking of the coming Messiah, John the Baptist said,

> ...after me will come one who is more powerful than I, whose
> sandals I am not fit to carry. He will baptize you with the Holy
> Spirit and with fire (Matthew 3:11).

This was a promise that Jesus would baptize His followers with the Holy
Spirit.

WHO IS THE HOLY SPIRIT?

1. The Holy Spirit is a personality; He is not just an impersonal force,
   power or influence. This is seen by the following:

Personal pronouns are always used when speaking of Him. In other
words, the pronouns "He," "Him" or "Himself" are used and not "it."
The Holy Spirit is not a thing; He has personality. The Holy Spirit
possesses attributes of personality such as wisdom and knowledge
(Acts 15:28; 1 Cor. 2:10-12). He has a "mind" or purpose (Rom. 8:27).
He "determines" to do things (1 Cor. 12:11). He can be "grieved"
(Eph. 4:30). He teaches (John 14:26), and He convicts the world of sin
(John 16:8). He appoints, commissions and commands (Acts 13:2;
20:28). Furthermore, the Holy Spirit is said to speak (John 16:13; Acts
1:16; 13:2; Rev. 3:22). All of these qualities could not be attributes of
a mere impersonal force or power but only a personality.

2. The Holy Spirit is God. He is equal with God and one with God.

Several triune Scriptures equate the Holy Spirit with God (Matthew 28:19; 2 Cor. 13:14; 1 Pet. 1:2). Several Scriptures call the Holy Spirit "God":

> **Acts 5:3-4** (NKJV) [3] But Peter said, "Ananias, why has Satan filled your heart to lie to the Holy Spirit and keep back *part* of the price of the land for yourself? [4] While it remained, was it not your own? And after it was sold, was it not in your own control? Why have you conceived this thing in your heart? You have not lied to men but to God."

> **1 Corinthians 3:16-17** (NKJV) [16] Do you not know that you are the temple of God and *that* the Spirit of God dwells in you? [17] If anyone defiles the temple of God, God will destroy him. For the temple of God is holy, which *temple* you are.

> Cf. 1 Cor. 12:4-6; Eph. 2:22

> The Holy Spirit possesses Divine attributes. The Scriptures reveal the Holy Spirit as omnipresent (Psalm 139:7-10), omniscient (1 Cor. 2:10-11) and omnipotent (Gen. 1:2).

EXPLANATION AND SCRIPTURAL BASIS

A. The Traditional Pentecostal Understanding

The topic of this chapter has become important today because many Christians say they have experienced a "baptism in the Holy Spirit" that came after they became Christians and that brought great blessing in their lives. They claim that prayer and Bible study have become more meaningful and effective, that they have discovered new joy in worship, and they often say that they have received new spiritual gifts (especially and most frequently, the gift of speaking in tongues).

This traditional Pentecostal or charismatic position is supported from Scripture in the following way:

- Jesus' disciples were born-again believers long before the day of Pentecost, perhaps during Jesus' life and ministry, but certainly by the time that Jesus, after His resurrection, *"breathed on them, and said to them, 'Receive the Holy Spirit'"* (John 20:22).

- Jesus nevertheless commanded His disciples *"not to depart from Jerusalem, but to wait for the promise of the Father"* (Acts 1:4), telling them, *"Before many days you shall be baptized with the Holy Spirit"* (Acts 1:5). He told them, *"You shall receive power when the Holy Spirit has come upon you"* (Acts 1:8). The disciples then obeyed Jesus' command and waited in Jerusalem for the Holy Spirit to come upon them so that they would receive new empowering for witness and ministry.

- When the disciples had waited for ten days, the days of Pentecost came, tongues of fire rested above their heads, "And they were all filled with the Holy Spirit and began to speak in other tongues, as the Spirit gave them utterance" (Acts 2:4). This clearly shows that they received a baptism in (or with) the Holy Spirit. Although the disciples were born again long before Pentecost, at Pentecost they received a "baptism with the Holy Spirit" (Acts 1:5 and 11:16 refer to it this way) that was subsequent to conversion and resulted in great empowering for ministry as well as speaking in tongues.

- Christians today, like the apostles, should ask Jesus for a "baptism in the Holy Spirit" and thus follow the pattern of the disciples' lives. If we receive this baptism in the Holy Spirit, it will result in much more power for ministry for our own lives, just as it did in the lives of the disciples, and will often (or always, according to some teachers) result in speaking in tongues as well.

- Support for this pattern – in which people are first born again and then later are baptized in the Holy Spirit – is seen in several other instances in the book of Acts. It is seen, for example, in Acts 8, where the people of Samaria first became Christians when they "believed Philip as he preached good news about the kingdom of God and the name of Jesus Christ" (Acts 8:12), but only later received the Holy Spirit when the apostles Peter and John came from Jerusalem and prayed for them (Acts 8:14-17).

Another example of this is found in Acts 19, where Paul came and found "some disciples" at Ephesus (Acts 19:1). But, "when Paul had laid his hands upon them, the Holy Spirit came on them; and they spoke with tongues and prophesized" (Acts 19:6).

All of these examples (Acts 2, 8, sometimes 10, and 19) are cited by Pentecostals in order to show that a "baptism in the Holy Spirit" subsequent to conversion was a very common occurrence for New Testament Christians. Therefore, they reason, if it was common for Christians in Acts to have this second experience sometime after conversion, should it not be common for us today as well?

We can analyze this issue of the baptism in the Holy Spirit by asking three questions: (1) What does the phrase "baptism in the Holy Spirit" mean in the New Testament? (2) How should we understand the "second experiences" that came to born-again believers in the book of Acts? (3) Are there other biblical expressions, such as "filling with the Holy Spirit," that are better suited to describe an empowering with the Holy Spirit that comes after conversion?

B. What Does "Baptism in the Holy Spirit" Mean in the New Testament?

There are only seven passages in the New Testament where we read of someone being baptized in the Holy Spirit. (The English translations quoted here use the word *with* rather than *in*.) The seven passages are as follows:

In the first four verses, John the Baptist is speaking of Jesus and predicting that He will baptize (people) in/with the Holy Spirit:

> **Matthew 3:11** "I baptize you with water for repentance, but he who is coming after me is mightier that I, whose sandals I am not worthy to carry; he will *baptize you with the Holy Spirit* and with fire."

> **Mark 1:8** "I have baptized you with water; but he will *baptize you with the Holy Spirit.*"

> **Luke 3:16** "I baptize you with water; but he who is mightier that I is coming, the thong of his sandals I am not worthy to untie; he will *baptize you with the Holy Spirit* and with fire.'"

> **John 1:33** "He who sent me to baptize with water said to me, 'He on whom you see the Spirit descend and remain, this is he who *baptizes with the Holy Spirit.*'"

The next two passages refer directly to Pentecost:

> **Acts 1:5** [Here Jesus says,] "John baptized with water, but before many days you shall be *baptized with the Holy Spirit.*"

> **Acts 11:16** [Here Peter refers back to the same words of Jesus that were quoted in the previous verse. He says,] "I remembered the word of the Lord, how he said, 'John baptized with water, but you shall be *baptized with the Holy Spirit.*'"

These two passages show us that whatever we may understand baptism in the Holy Spirit to be, it certainly happened at the day of Pentecost as recorded in Acts 2, when the Holy Spirit fell in great power on the disciples and those with them, and they spoke in other tongues, and about three thousand people were converted (Acts 2:14).

It is important to realize that all six of these verses use almost exactly the same expression in Greek, with the only differences being some variation in word order or verb tense to fit the sentence, and with one example having the preposition understood rather than expressed explicitly.

The only remaining reference in the New Testament is in the Pauline epistles:

> **1 Corinthians 12:13** (NIV) "For we were all *baptized in one Spirit into one body* – whether Jews or Greeks, slave or free – and we were all given the one Spirit to drink."

Now the question is whether 1 Corinthians 12:13 refers to the same activity as these other six verses. In many English translations it appears to be different, for many translations are similar to the RSV, which says, "For *by one Spirit* we were all baptized into one body." Those who support the Pentecostal view of baptism in the Holy Spirit after conversion are quite eager to see this verse as referring to something other than baptism in the Holy Spirit, and they frequently emphasize the difference that comes out in the English translations. In all the other six verses, Jesus is the one who baptizes people and the Holy Spirit is the "element" (parallel to water in physical baptism) in which or with which Jesus baptizes people. But here in 1 Corinthians 12:13 (so the Pentecostal explanation goes) we have something quite different – here the person doing the baptizing is not Jesus but the Holy Spirit. Therefore, they say, 1 Corinthians 12:13 should not be taken into account when we ask what the New Testament means by "baptism in the Holy Spirit."

This point is very important to the Pentecostal position, because, if we admit that 1 Corinthians 12:13 refers to baptism *in* the Holy Spirit, then it is very hard to maintain that it is an experience that comes after conversion. In this verse Paul says that this baptism in/with/by the Holy Spirit made us members of the body of Christ – "We were all baptized *in* one Spirit into one body" (1 Cor. 12:13 NIV). But if this really is a "baptism in the Holy Spirit," the same as the event that was referred to in the previous six verses, then Paul is saying that it happened to all the Corinthians *when they became members of the body of Christ; that is, when they became Christians*. For it was that baptism that resulted in their being members of the body of Christ, the church. Such a conclusion would be very difficult for the Pentecostal position that holds that baptism in the Holy Spirit is something that occurs after conversion, not at the same time.

Is it possible to sustain the Pentecostal view that the other six verses refer to a baptism *by Jesus* in which He baptizes us in (or with) the Holy Spirit, but that 1 Corinthians 12:13 refers to something different, to a baptism *by the Holy Spirit*? Although the distinction seems to make sense from some English translations, it really cannot be supported by an examination of the Greek text, for there the expression is almost identical to the expressions we have seen in the other six verses. Paul says, *en hene pneumatic...ebaptisthemen* ("in one Spirit...we were baptized"). Apart from one small difference (he refers to "one Spirit" rather than "the Holy Spirit"), all the other elements are the same: the verb is *baptizo*, and the prepositional phrase contains the same words (*en* plus the dative noun *pneumatic*). If we translate this same Greek expression "baptize *in* the Holy Spirit" (or "baptize with the Holy Spirit") in the other six New Testament occurrences where we find it, then it seems only proper that we translate it the same here. It seems hard to deny that the original readers would have seen this phrase as referring to the same thing as the other six verses, because for them the words were the same.

But why have modern English translations translated this verse to say, "By one Spirit we were all baptized into one body," thus giving apparent support to the Pentecostal interpretation? We should first note that the NASB gives "in" as a marginal translation, and the NIV margin gives both "with" and "in" as alternatives. The reason these translations have chosen the word "by" has apparently been a desire to avoid an appearance of two locations for the baptism in the same sentence. The sentence already says that this baptism was "into one body," and perhaps the translators thought it seemed awkward to say, "*in* one Spirit we were all baptized *into* one body." But this should be seen as a great difficulty, for Paul says, referring to the Israelites, "all were baptized *into* Moses *in* the cloud and *in* the sea" (1 Cor. 10:2) – a closely parallel expression where the cloud and the sea are the "elements" that surrounded or overwhelmed the people of Israel and *Moses* means the new life of participation in the Mosaic covenant and the fellowship of God's people (led by Moses) that the Israelites found themselves in after they had passed through the cloud and the sea. It is not that there were two locations for the same baptism, but one was the element in which they were baptized and the other was the location in which they found themselves after the baptism. This is very similar to 1 Corinthians 12:13: the Holy Spirit was the *element* in which they were baptized, and the body of Christ, the church, was the *location* in which they found themselves after that baptism. It thus seems appropriate to conclude that 1 Corinthians 12:13 also refers to baptism "in" or "with" the Holy Spirit, and is referring to the same thing as the other six verses mentioned.

But this has a significant implication for us: it means that, as far as the apostle Paul was concerned, *baptism in the Holy Spirit occurred at conversion*. He says that all the Corinthians were baptized in the Holy Spirit and the results were that they became members of the body of Christ: "For we were all baptized in one Spirit into one body" (1 Cor. 12:13 NIV). "Baptism in the Holy Spirit," therefore, must refer to the activity of the Holy Spirit at the beginning of the Christian life when He gives us new spiritual life (in regeneration) and cleanses us and gives a clear break with the power and love of sin (the initial stage of sanctification). In this way "baptism in the Holy Spirit" refers to all that the Holy Spirit does at the beginning of our Christian lives. But this means that it cannot refer to an experience after conversion, as the Pentecostal interpretation would have it.

But how, then, do we understand the references to baptism in the Holy Spirit in Acts 1:5 and 11:6, both of which refer to the day of Pentecost? Were these not instances where the disciples, having previously been regenerated by the Holy Spirit, now experienced a new empowering from the Holy Spirit that enabled them to minister effectively?

It is true that the disciples were "born again" long before Pentecost, and in fact probably long before Jesus breathed on them and told them to receive the Holy Spirit in John 20:22. Jesus had said, "No one can come to Me unless the Father who sent Me draws him" (John 6:44), but the disciples certainly had come to Jesus and had followed Him (even though their understanding of who He was increased gradually over time). Certainly when Peter said to Jesus, "You are the Christ, the Son of the living God" (Matt. 16:16), it was evidence of some kind of regenerating work of the Holy Spirit in his heart. Jesus told him, "Flesh and blood has not revealed this to you, but My Father who is in heaven" (Matt. 16:17). And Jesus had said to the Father regarding His disciples, "I have given them the words which you have given Me, and *they have received them* and know in truth that I came from You; and they have believed that You sent Me...*I have guarded them*, and *none of them is lost* but the son of perdition, that the scripture might be fulfilled" (John 17:8, 12). The disciples had "little faith" (Matt. 8:26) at times, but they did have faith! Certainly they were regenerated long before the day of Pentecost.

But we must realize that the day of Pentecost is much more than an individual event in the lives of Jesus' disciples and those with them. The day of Pentecost was the point of transition between the old covenant work and ministry of the Holy Spirit and the new covenant work and ministry of the Holy Spirit. Of course the Holy Spirit was at work throughout the Old Testament, hovering over the waters of the first day of creation (Gen. 1:2), empowering people for service to God and leadership and prophecy (Ex. 31:3; 35:31; Deut. 34:9; Judg. 14:6; 1 Sam. 16:13; Ps. 51:11, et al.). But during that time the work of the Holy Spirit in individual lives was, in general, a work of lesser power.

There are several indications of a less powerful and less extensive work of the Holy Spirit in the old covenant: the Holy Spirit only came to a few people with significant power for ministry (Num. 11:16-17, for example), but Moses longed for the day when the Holy Spirit would be poured out on all of God's people: "Would that all the Lord's people were prophets, that the Lord would put His spirit upon them!" (Num. 11:29). The equipping of the Holy Spirit for special ministries could be lost, as it was in the life of Saul (1 Sam. 16:14), and as David feared that it might be in his own life (Ps. 51:11). In terms of spiritual power in the lives of the people of God, there was little power over the dominion of Satan, resulting in very little effective evangelism of the nations around Israel, and no examples of ability to cast out demons. The old covenant work of the Holy Spirit was almost completely confined to the nation of Israel, but in the new covenant there is created a new "dwelling place of God" (Eph. 2:22), the church, which unites both Gentiles and Jews in the body of Christ.

Moreover, the Old Testament people of God looked forward to a "new covenant" age when the work of the Holy Spirit would be much more powerful and much more widespread (Num. 11:29; Jer. 31:31-33; Ezek. 36:26-27; Joel 2:28-29). Of course, there were examples in the Old Testament where certain leaders were remarkably gifted by God and empowered by the Holy Spirit – Moses, David, Daniel, many of the writing prophets, and even Samson received unusual empowering from the Holy Spirit for specific ministries. But their experiences were not typical of the vast numbers of God's people who were saved by faith as they looked forward to the promised Messiah's coming, but who did not have the outpouring of the Holy Spirit in the new covenant power that we experience today.

When the New Testament opens, we see John the Baptist as the last of the Old Testament prophets. Jesus said, "Among those born of women there has risen no one greater than John the Baptist; yet he who is least in the kingdom of heaven is greater than he...all the prophets and the law

116

prophesied until John; and if you are willing to accept it, he is Elijah who is to come" (Matt. 11:11-14). John knew that he baptized with water, but Jesus would baptize with the Holy Spirit (John 3:16). John the Baptist, then, still was living in an "old covenant" experience of the working of the Holy Spirit.

In the life of Jesus, we first see the new covenant power of the Holy Spirit at work. The Holy Spirit descends on him at His baptism (Luke 3:21-22), and after His temptation Jesus "returned *in the power of the Spirit* into Galilee" (Luke 4:14). Then we begin to see what this new covenant power of the Holy Spirit will look like, because Jesus casts out demons with a word, heals all who are brought to Him, and teaches with authority that people had not heard before (see Luke 4:16-44, et al.).

The disciples, however, do not receive this full new covenant empowering for ministry until the Day of Pentecost, for Jesus tells them to wait in Jerusalem, and promises, *"You shall receive power* when the Holy Spirit has come upon you" (Acts 1:8). This was a transition in the lives of the disciples as well (see John 7:39; 14:17; 16:7; Acts 2:16). The promise of Joel that the Holy Spirit would come in new covenant fullness was fulfilled (Acts 2:16) as Jesus returned to heaven and then was given authority to pour out the Holy Spirit in new fullness and power (Acts 2:33).

What was the result in the lives of the disciples? These believers, who had had an old covenant less-powerful experience of the Holy Spirit in their lives, received on the Day of Pentecost a more-powerful new-covenant experience of the Holy Spirit working in their lives. They received much greater "power" (Acts 1:8), power for living the Christian life and for carrying out Christian ministry.

This new covenant power gave the disciples more effectiveness in their witness and their ministry (Acts 1:8; Eph. 4:8, 11-13), much greater power for victory over the influence of sin in the lives of all believers (note the emphasis on the power of Christ's resurrection at work within us in Rom.

6:11-14; 8:13-14; Gal. 2:20; Phil. 3:10), and power for victory over Satan and demonic forces that would attack believers (2 Cor. 10:3-4; Eph. 1:9-21; 6:10-18; 1 John 4:4). This new covenant power of the Holy Spirit also resulted in a wide and hitherto unknown distribution of gifts for ministry to all believers (Acts 2:16-18; 1 Cor. 12:7, 11; 1 Peter 4:10; cf. Num. 11:17, 24-29). These gifts also had corporate implications because they were intended not to be used individualistically but for the corporate building up of the body of Christ (1 Cor. 12:7; 14:12). It also meant that the gospel was no longer effectively limited to the Jews only, but that all races and all nations would hear the gospel in power and would be united into the church, to the glory of God (Eph. 2:11-3:10). The Day of Pentecost was certainly a remarkable time of transition in the whole history of the world, because on that day the Holy Spirit began to function among God's people with new covenant power.

But this fact helps us understand what happened to the disciples at Pentecost. They received this remarkable new empowering from the Holy Spirit *because they were living at the time of the transition between the old covenant work of the Holy Spirit and the new covenant work of the Holy Spirit.* Though it was a "second experience" of the Holy Spirit, coming as it did long after their conversion, it is not to be taken as a pattern for us, for we are not living at a time of transition in the work of the Holy Spirit. In their case, believers with an old covenant empowering from the Holy Spirit became believers with a new covenant empowering from the Holy Spirit. But we today do not first become believers with a weaker, old covenant work of the Holy Spirit in our hearts and wait until some later time to receive a new covenant work of the Holy Spirit. Rather, we are in the same position as those who became Christians in the church at Corinth: when we became Christians we are all *"baptized in one Spirit into one body"* (1 Cor. 12:13) – just as the Corinthians were, and just as were the new believers in many churches who were converted when Paul traveled on his missionary journeys.

In conclusion, the disciples certainly did experience "a baptism in the Holy

Spirit" after conversion on the Day of Pentecost, but this happened because they were living at a unique point in history, and this event in their lives is therefore not a pattern that we are to seek to imitate.

What shall we say about the phrase "baptism in the Holy Spirit"? It is a phrase that the New Testament authors use to speak of coming into the new covenant power of the Holy Spirit. It happened at Pentecost for the disciples, but it happened at conversion for the Corinthians and for us.

It is not a phrase the New Testament authors would use to speak of any post-conversion experience of empowering by the Holy Spirit.

C.   How Should We Understand the "Second Experiences" in Acts?"

But even if we have correctly understood the experience of the disciples at Pentecost as recorded in Acts 2, are there not other examples of people who had a "second experience" of empowering of the Holy Spirit after conversion, such as those in Acts 8 (at Samaria), Acts 10 (Cornelius' household), and Acts 19 (the Ephesian disciples)?

These are not really convincing examples to prove the Pentecostal doctrine of baptism in the Holy Spirit either. First, the expression "baptism in the Holy Spirit" is not ordinarily used to refer to any of these events, and this should give us some hesitation in applying this phrase to them. But more importantly, a closer look at each case shows more clearly what was happening in these events.

In Acts 8:4-25 the Samaritan people "believed Philip as he preached good news about the kingdom of God and the name of Jesus Christ" and "they were baptized, both men and women" (Acts 8:12). Some have argued that this was not genuine saving faith on the part of the Samaritans. However, there is no indication in the text that Philip had a deficient understanding of the gospel (he had been prominent in the Jerusalem church) or that Philip himself thought that their faith in Christ was inadequate, for he allowed them to be baptized (Acts 8:12).

A better understanding of this event would be that God, in His providence, sovereignly waited to give the new covenant empowering of the Holy Spirit to the Samaritans directly through the hands of the apostles (Acts 8:14-17) so that it might be evident to the highest leadership in the Jerusalem church that the Samaritans were not second-class citizens but full members of the church. This was important because of the historical animosity between Jews and Samaritans ("Jews have no dealings with Samaritans," John 4:9), and because Jesus had specified that the spread of the gospel to Samaria would be the next major step after it had been preached in Jerusalem and the region of Judea that surrounded Jerusalem: "You shall be My witnesses in Jerusalem and in all Judea *and Samaria* and to the end of the earth" (Acts 1:8). Thus, the event in Acts 8 was a kind of "Samaritan Pentecost," a special outpouring of the Holy Spirit on the people of Samaria, who were a mixed race of Jewish and Gentile ancestry, so that it might be evident to all that the full new covenant blessings and power of the Holy Spirit had come to this group of people as well, and were not confined to Jews only. Because this is a special event in the history of redemption, as the pattern of Acts 1:8 is worked out in the book of Acts, it is not a pattern for us to repeat today. It is simply part of the transition between the old covenant experience of the Holy Spirit and the new covenant experience of the Holy Spirit.

The situation in Acts 10 is less complicated, because it is not even clear that Cornelius was a genuine believer before Peter came and preached the gospel to him. Certainly he had not trusted in Christ for salvation. He is rather a Gentile who was one of the first examples of the way in which the gospel would go "to the end of the earth" (Acts 1:8). Certainly Cornelius had not first believed in Christ's death and resurrection to save him and then later come into a second experience after his conversion.

In Acts 19, once again we encounter a situation of some people who had not really heard the gospel of salvation through Christ. They had been baptized into the baptism of John the Baptist (Acts 19:3), so they were probably people who had heard John the Baptist preach, or had talked to others who had heard John the Baptist preach, and had been baptized "into John's baptism" (Acts 19:3) as a sign that they were repenting of their sins and preparing for the Messiah who was to come. They certainly had not heard of Christ's death and resurrection, for they had not even heard that there was a Holy Spirit (Acts 19:2)! – a fact that no one who was present at Pentecost or who had heard the gospel after Pentecost could have failed to know. It is likely that they had not even heard that Jesus had come and lived and died, because Paul had to explain to them, "John baptized with the baptism of repentance, telling the people to believe in the one who was to come after him, *that is Jesus*" (Acts 19:4). Therefore these "disciples" in Ephesus did not have new covenant understanding or new covenant faith, and they certainly did not have a new covenant empowering of the Holy Spirit – they were "disciples" only in the sense of followers of John the Baptist who were still waiting for the Messiah. When they heard of him they believed in him, and then received the power of the Holy Spirit that was appropriate to the gospel of the risen Lord Jesus Christ.

Because of this, these disciples at Ephesus are certainly not a pattern for us today either, for we do not first have faith in a Messiah that we are waiting for, and then later learn that Jesus has come and lived and died and risen again. We come into an understanding of the gospel of Christ immediately, and we, like the Corinthians, enter immediately into the new covenant experience of the power of the Holy Spirit.

It seems therefore that there are no New Testament texts that encourage us to seek for a second experience of "baptism in the Holy Spirit" that comes after conversion.

D. What Terms Shall We Use to Refer to an Empowering by the Holy Spirit That Comes After Conversion?

The previous sections have argued that "baptism in the Holy Spirit" is not the term the New Testament authors would use to speak of a post-conversion work of the Spirit, and that the examples of "second experiences" of receiving the Holy Spirit in the book of Acts are not patterns for us to imitate in our Christian lives. But the question remains, What is actually happening to the millions of people who claim that they have received this 'baptism in the Holy Spirit' and that it has brought much blessing to their lives? Could it be that this has been a genuine work of the Holy Spirit but that the biblical categories, expressions and teachings that point to this kind of work of the Holy Spirit after conversion need to be understood more accurately? I think this is the case. It is appropriate to comment on the importance of having a correct understanding at this point.

1. **Harm Comes to the Church From Teaching Two-Class Christianity.**

At various times in the history of the church Christians have attempted to divide the church into two categories of believers. This is in effect what happens with the Pentecostal doctrine of baptism in the Holy Spirit. It could be pictured with the world divided between Christians and Non-Christians, and then picturing the Christians divided between two categories of ordinary believers and Spirit-baptized believers.

But such a division of Christian into two categories is not a unique understanding that is found only in Pentecostal teaching in the twentieth century. In fact, much Pentecostal teaching came out of earlier holiness groups that had taught that Christians could either be ordinary believers or "sanctified" believers. Other groups have divided Christians using different categories, such as ordinary believers and those who are "Spirit filled," or ordinary believers and those who are "disciples," or "carnal" and "spiritual" Christians. In fact, the Roman Catholic Church had long had not two, but three, categories: ordinary believers, priests, and saints.

Although those who teach the classical Pentecostal view of baptism in the Holy Spirit may deny that they are attempting to divide Christians into two categories, such a division is implicit every time they ask whether someone has been baptized in the Holy Spirit or not. Such a question strongly suggests that there are two groups of Christians, those who have had this experience of "baptism in the Holy Spirit" and those who have not.

What is the problem with viewing Christians as existing in two categories like this? The problem is that it contributes to a "we-they" mentality in churches, and leads to jealousy, pride, and divisiveness. No matter how much these people who have received this special empowering of the Holy Spirit try to be thoughtful and considerate of those who have not, if they genuinely love their fellow brothers and sisters in Christ, and if this has been a very helpful experience in their own Christian lives, they cannot help but give the impression that they would like others to share this experience as well. Even if they are not proud in their hearts (and it seems to me that most are not) with respect to this experience, such a conviction that there is a second category of Christians will inevitably give an impression of pride or spiritual superiority. Yet there will very likely be a sense of jealously on the part of those who have not had such an experience. In this way, a view of two groups within the church is fostered, and the repeated charge of divisiveness that is made against the charismatic movement is given some credibility. In fact, divisions often do occur in churches.

The major objection to this position is that the New Testament itself teaches no such two-level or two-class Christianity. Nowhere in the Epistles do we read of Paul or Peter telling a church that is having problems, "You all need to be baptized in the Holy Spirit." Nowhere do we hear of the risen Lord Jesus speaking to the troubled and weak churches in Revelation 2-3, "Ask me to baptize you in the Holy Spirit." It is hard to avoid the conclusion that the two-level or two-class view taught by all of these groups throughout history does not have a solid foundation in the New Testament itself.

2. There Are Many Degrees of Empowering, Fellowship With God, and Personal Christian Maturity.

Is there a better model for understanding the varying degrees of maturity and power and fellowship with God that Christians experience? If we are willing to eliminate the categories that make us think of Christians in one group or another, a better model is possible.

Christians are not divided into categories or set groups. Rather, there are Christians at all points along a scale of increasing Christian maturity (sanctification), increasing closeness of fellowship in their walk with God (an aspect of adoption), and greater experiences of the power of the Holy Spirit at work in their lives and ministries.

The Christian life should be one of growth in all of these areas as we progress throughout our lives. For many people that growth will be gradual and progressive and will extend over all the years of their lives.

a. How Should We Understand Contemporary Experience

What then has happened to people who say they have experienced a "baptism in the Holy Spirit" that has brought great blessing to their lives? We must understand first what is commonly taught about the need to prepare for baptism in the Holy Spirit. Very often people will be taught that they should confess all known sins, repent of any remaining sin in their lives, trust Christ to forgive those sins, commit every area of their lives to the Lord's service, yield themselves fully to Him, and believe that Christ is going to empower them in a new way and equip them with new gifts for ministry. Then after that preparation, they are encouraged to ask Jesus in prayer to baptize them in the Holy Spirit. But what does the preparation do? It is a guaranteed prescription for significant growth in the Christian life! Such a confession, repentance, renewed commitment, and heightened faith and expectation, if they are genuine, can only bring positive results in a person's life. If any Christian is sincere in these steps of preparation to receive baptism in the Holy Spirit, there will certainly be growth in sanctification and deeper fellowship with God. In addition to that, we may expect that at many of these times the Holy Spirit will graciously bring a measure of the additional fullness and empowering that sincere Christians are seeking, even though their theological understanding and vocabulary may be imperfect in the asking. If this happens, they may well realize increased power for ministry and growth in spiritual gifts as well. We could say that this person has made a large step forward in their Christian life.

Of course prayer and Bible study and worship will seem more meaningful. Of course there will be more fruitfulness in evangelism and other kinds of ministry. But it is important to recognize that someone who moves from one place of maturity and experience to another is not in a separate category of Christians, such as a group of those who have been "baptized in the Holy Spirit" and those who are therefore different from those who have not had such an experience. There might be another Christian in the same church who has never had such a large step of growth, but who has nonetheless been making steady progress for the last forty years of his or her Christian life and has come to a greater level of maturity and faithfulness. Although the first example may have grown in maturity and experience, certainly farther along than he or she was before, this is certainly a positive result in his or her life. Thus, with this understanding of the Christian life, we have no divisions of Christians into two categories.

Before we leave this topic, one more observation should be made: in many cases the charismatic movement has brought teaching on the baptism of the Holy Spirit into more liberal churches where, for many years, there has not been a clear proclamation of the gospel of salvation by faith in Christ alone, and where people have not been taught that they can believe the Bible completely as God's Word to us. In such cases, many of the people in those churches have never experienced saving faith and therefore are actually non-Christians and not born again. Now when a representative of the charismatic renewal comes to these churches and tells them that they can experience new vitality in their Christian lives, and then tells them that the preparation is to repent of all known sins, ask Christ for forgiveness of those sins and trust Him to forgive them, and commit their lives totally to Christ as their Lord, they eagerly respond to those directions. Then they pray and ask Jesus to baptize them in the Holy Spirit. The actual result is that they become Christians because of their sincerity and deep eagerness to draw closer to God. While they think that they have been baptized by the Holy Spirit as a second experience in their Christian lives, what has in fact happened is that they have become Christians for the first time. (They have been "baptized in the Holy Spirit" in the true New Testament sense!) The next day it is almost impossible to keep them silent, they are so excited. Suddenly reading the Bible has become meaningful. Suddenly prayer has become real. Suddenly they know the presence of God in their lives. Suddenly worship has become an experience of deep joy, and often they have begun to experience spiritual gifts that they had not known before. It is no wonder that the charismatic renewal has brought such excitement (and often much controversy) to many Roman Catholic parishes and to many mainline, more liberal Protestant denominations. Though we may differ with the way this teaching is actually presented, no one should fault the good results that have come about as a result of it in these churches.

b. What Terms Should We Use Today?

Now we can understand why our use of terms to describe this experience and the category of understanding we put it in are so important. If we use the traditional Pentecostal terminology of "baptism of the Holy Spirit," then we almost inevitably end up with two-category Christianity, for this is seen as a common experience that *can* and indeed *should* happen to Christians at one point in time, and, once it has happened, does not need to be repeated. It is seen as a single experience of empowering for ministry that is distinct from the experiencing of becoming a Christian, and people either have received that experience or they have not. Especially when the experience is described in terms of

126

what happened to the disciples at Pentecost in Acts 2 (which was clearly a one-time experience for them), the Samaritans in Acts 8, and the Ephesian disciples in Acts 19, it is clearly implied that this is a one-time event that empowers people for ministry but that also puts them in a separate category or group than the one they were in before this experience. The use of the term "*the* baptism in the Holy Spirit" inevitably implies two groups of Christians.

But if we are correct in understanding the experience that has come to millions of people in the charismatic renewal as a large step of growth in their Christian lives, then some other term than "baptism in the Holy Spirit" would seem to be more appropriate. There might be several terms that we could use, so long as they allow for repetition, varying degrees of intensity, and further development beyond that one experienced, and so long as they do not suggest that all truly obedient Christians should have the same experience. We have already used one expression, "*a large step of growth* in several aspects of the Christian life." Because this phrase speaks of "a large step of growth" it cannot be misunderstood to refer to a single experience that puts Christians in a new category. And because it is referred to as a large step of growth, it clearly implies that others may experience such growth in smaller steps over a longer period of time, but reach the same point in the Christian life.

Another term that may be helpful is "a new *empowering for ministry*." It is certainly true that many who have received such a charismatic experience do find new power for ministry in their Christian lives, including the ability to use spiritual gifts that had not been theirs before. However, the problem with this phrase is that it does not say anything about the deepened fellowship with God, the greater effectiveness in prayer and Bible study, and the new joy in worship that often also results from this experience.

c. What is "Being Filled With the Spirit"?

Yet an even more commonly used term in the New Testament is *"being filled with the Holy Spirit."* Because of its frequent use in contexts that speak of Christian growth and ministry, *this seems to me to be the best term to use* to describe genuine "second experiences" today (or third or fourth experiences, etc.). Paul tells the Ephesians, "Do not get drunk with wine, for that is debauchery; but *be filled with the Spirit*" (Eph. 5:18). He uses a present tense imperative verb that could more explicitly be translated, "Be continually being filled with the Holy Spirit," thus implying that this is something that should repeatedly be happening to Christians. Such fullness of the Holy Spirit will result in *renewed worship and thanksgiving* (Eph. 5:19-20), and in renewed relationships to others, especially those in authority over us or those under our authority (Eph. 5:21-6:9). In addition, since the Holy Spirit is the Spirit who sanctifies us, such a filling will often result in *increased sanctification*. Furthermore, since the Holy Spirit is the one who empowers us for Christian service and gives us spiritual gifts, such filling will often result in *increased power for ministry* and increased effectiveness and perhaps diversity in the use of *spiritual gifts*.

We see examples of repeated filling with the Holy Spirit in the book of Acts. In Acts 2:4, the disciples and those with them are "all *filled with the Holy Spirit*." Later, when Peter was standing before the Sanhedrin, we read, "Then Peter, *filled with the Holy Spirit*, said to them . . ." (Acts 4:8). But a little later, when Peter and the other apostles had returned to the church to tell what had happened (Acts 4:23), they joined together in prayer. After they had prayed they were again filled with the Holy Spirit, a sequence of events that Luke makes clear: "*After* they prayed, the place where they were meeting was shaken. And they were all *filled with the Holy Spirit* and spoke the word of God boldly" (Acts 4:31 NIV). Even though Peter had been filled with the Holy Spirit at Pentecost (Acts 2:4), he had later been filled with the Holy Spirit before speaking to the Sanhedrin (Acts 4:8). He was once again filled with the Holy Spirit after the group of Christians he was meeting with had prayed.

Therefore, it is appropriate to understand filling with the Holy Spirit *not as a one-time event* but as *an event that can occur over and over again* in a Christian's life. It may involve a momentary empowering for a specific ministry (such as apparently happened in Acts 4:8; 7:55), but it may also refer to a long-term characteristic of a person's life (see Acts 6:3; 11:24). In either case such filling can occur many times in a person's life: even though Stephen, as an early deacon (or apostolic assistant), was a man "full of the Spirit and of wisdom" (Acts 6:3, 5), when he was being stoned he apparently received a fresh new filling of the Holy Spirit in great power (Acts 7:55).

Someone might object that a person who is already "full" of the Holy Spirit cannot become more full — if a glass is full of water no more water can be put into it. But a water glass is a poor analogy for us as real people, for God is able to cause us to grow and to be able to contain much more of the Holy Spirit's fullness and power. A better analogy might be a balloon, which can be "full" of air even though it has very little air in it. When more air is blown in, the balloon expands and there is a sense it is "fuller." So it is with us: we can be filled with the Holy Spirit and at the same time be able to receive much more of the Holy Spirit as well. It was only Jesus Himself to whom the Father gave the Spirit without measure (John 3:34).

The divisiveness that comes with the term *"baptism in the Holy Spirit"* could easily be avoided by using any of the alternative terms mentioned in this section. People could be thankful for "a new fullness of the Holy Spirit" or "a new empowering for ministry" or "a significant step in growth" in some aspect of another Christian's life. There would be no separating into "we" and "they," for we would recognize that we are all part of one body with no separate categories. In fact, many charismatics and even some traditional Pentecostals today are using the term "baptism in the Holy Spirit" far less frequently, preferring to use other terms such as "being filled with the Holy Spirit" instead.

Moreover, many people who have had no single dramatic experience (such as what Pentecostals have called a baptism in the Holy Spirit) have nonetheless begun to experience new freedom and joy in worship (often with the advent of modern worship and praise songs in their churches), and to use a wider variety of spiritual gifts such as healing, prophecy, working of miracles, discernment of spirits, and the ability to exercise authority over demonic forces with prayer and a word of rebuke spoken directly to the evil spirits. Sometimes the gift of speaking in tongues and the gift of interpretation have been used as well, but in other cases they have not. All of this is to say that the differences between Pentecostals and charismatics on the one hand, and more traditional and mainstream evangelical Christians on the other hand, seem to me to be breaking down more and more, and there are fewer and fewer differences between them.

Someone may object that it is specifically this experience of praying for a baptism in the Holy Spirit that catapults people into a new level of power in ministry and effectiveness in use of spiritual gifts. Since this experience had been so helpful in the lives of millions of people, should we so quickly dismiss it? In response, it must be said that, if terminology "baptism in the Holy Spirit" is changed for something more representative of New Testament teaching, there should be no objection at all to people coming into churches, and to encouraging people to prepare their hearts for spiritual renewal by sincere repentance and renewed commitment to Christ and by believing that the Holy Spirit can work much more powerfully in their lives. There is nothing wrong with teaching people to pray and to seek this greater infilling of the Holy Spirit, or to expect and ask the Lord for an outpouring of more spiritual gifts in their lives, for the benefit of the body of Christ (see 1 Cor. 12:21; 14:1, 12). In fact, most evangelical Christians in every denomination genuinely long for greater power in ministry, greater joy in worship, and deeper fellowship with God. Many would also welcome increased understanding of spiritual gifts, and encouragement to grow in the use of them. If Pentecostal and charismatic Christians would be willing to teach on these things without the additional baggage of two-level Christianity that is implied by the term "baptism in the Holy Spirit," they might find a new era of greatly increased effectiveness in bringing teaching on these other areas of the Christian life to evangelicals generally.

3. **Being Filled With the Holy Spirit Does Not Always Result in Speaking in Tongues.**

One remaining point needs to be made with respect to the experience of being filled with the Holy Spirit. Because there were several cases in Acts where people received the new covenant power of the Holy Spirit and began to speak with tongues at the same time (Acts 2:4; 10:46; 19:6; probably also implied in 8:17-19 because of the parallel with the experience of the disciples in Acts 2), Pentecostal teaching has commonly maintained that the outward sign of baptism in the Holy Spirit is speaking in tongues (that is, speaking in languages that are not understood by and have not been learned by the person speaking, whether known human languages or other kinds of angelic or heavenly or miraculously given languages.)

But it important to realize that there are many cases where being filled with the Holy Spirit did not result in speaking in tongues. When Jesus was filled with the Holy Spirit in Luke 4:1, the result was strength to overcome the temptation of Satan in the wilderness. When the temptations were ended, and Jesus "returned in the power of the Spirit into Galilee" (Luke 4:14), the results were miracles of healing, casting out of demons, and teaching with authority. When Elizabeth was filled with the Holy Spirit, she spoke a word of blessing to Mark (Luke 1:41-45). When Zechariah was filled with the Holy Spirit, he prophesied (Luke 1:67-79). Other results of being filled with the Holy Spirit were powerful preaching of the gospel (Acts 4:31), (perhaps) wisdom and Christian maturity and sound judgment (Acts 6:3), powerful preaching and testimony when on trial (Acts 4:8), a vision of heaven (Acts 7:55), and (apparently) faith and maturity of life (Acts 11:24). Several of these cases may also imply the fullness of the Holy Spirit to empower some kind of ministry, especially in the context of the book of Acts, where the empowering of the Holy Spirit is frequently seen to result in miracles, preaching, and works of great power.

Therefore, while an experience of being filled with the Holy Spirit may result in the gift of speaking in tongues, or in the use of some other gifts that had not previously been experienced, it also may come without the gift of speaking in tongues. In fact, many Christians throughout history have experienced powerful infillings of the Holy Spirit that have not been accompanied by speaking in tongues. With regard to this gift as well as all other gifts, we must simply say that the Holy Spirit "apportions each one individually as he wills" (1 Cor. 12:11).

CHAPTER 9

BAPTISM OF SUFFERING

We talk so much about closed countries today that we have almost totally lost God's perspective on missions – as though He ever meant it to be safe and easy. There are no closed countries to those who assume that persecution, imprisonment, and death are the likely results of spreading the gospel.

> **Matthew 24:9** (NKJV) [9] "Then they will deliver you up to tribulation and kill you, and you will be hated by all nations for My name's sake.

> **John 15:20** (NKJV) [20] Remember the word that I said to you, 'A servant is not greater than his master.' If they persecuted Me, they will also persecute you. If they kept My word, they will keep yours also.

Until we recover God's perspective on suffering and the spread of the gospel, we will not rejoice in the triumphs of grace that He plans. Obedience in missions and social justice has always been costly, and always will be. God buried His Son on the mission field – and when He raised Him from the dead, He called the church to follow Him into the same dangerous field called "the world." But are we willing to follow?

We have, I fear, domesticated the concept of godliness into such inoffensive middle class morality and law-keeping that 2 Timothy 3:12 has become unintelligible to us.

> **2 Timothy 3:12** (NKJV) [12] Yes, and all who desire to live godly in Christ Jesus will suffer persecution.

I think that many of us are not prepared to suffer for the gospel. We should deal with this and find out what the Bible has to say about it. I believe that there are at least four Biblical purposes of suffering:

FOUR BIBLICAL PURPOSES OF SUFFERING

1. **The moral purpose**: Suffering refines our holiness and hope (Romans 5:1-8).
2. **The intimacy purpose**: In suffering, our relationship with Christ becomes deeper and sweeter (Philippians 3:7-14).
3. **The mission purpose**: God calls us to complete Christ's afflictions as we extend the worth of His through the reality of ours (Colossians 1:24).
4. **The glory purpose**: This slight, momentary affliction is working for us an eternal weight of glory (2 Corinthians 4:16-18).

THE MORAL PURPOSE

Romans 5:1-8 (NKJV) [1] Therefore, having been justified by faith, we have peace with God through our Lord Jesus Christ, [2] through whom also we have access by faith into this grace in which we stand, and rejoice in hope of the glory of God. [3] And not only *that,* but we also glory in tribulations, knowing that tribulation produces perseverance; [4] and perseverance, character; and character, hope. [5] Now hope does not disappoint, because the love of God has been poured out in our hearts by the Holy Spirit who was given to us. [6] For when we were still without strength, in due time Christ died for the ungodly. [7] For scarcely for a righteous man will one die; yet perhaps for a good man someone would even dare to die. [8] But God demonstrates His own love toward us, in that while we were still sinners, Christ died for us.

This scripture tells us that we should rejoice in the hope of the glory of God. But, what brings about this hope? Verse 3 and 4 describes what that is! Tribulations produce what we do, namely a stronger and stronger sense of hope which comes through the experience of patient perseverance and a sense of being approved.

God has purpose in the suffering of His people. That purpose is often different from the ministry goal that we are laboring for. God may not go about ministry productivity and efficiency at all the way we would. Again and again, Paul had to reckon with the strange work of God in His imprisonments and beatings and shipwrecks and broken plans. How could God be so inefficient as to let His mission be blocked like this again and again? The answer of this text (not the only answer) would be: God is committed to increasing the hope and holiness of His people in the process of reaching the lost. And only God knows how to balance those two things and bring them to pass in the best way.

THREE EFFECTS OF AFFLICTIONS

1. Perseverance

First, tribulations bring about perseverance, or patient endurance. Paul doesn't mean this is universally true. For many, tribulations unleash hatred and bitterness and anger and resentment and murmuring. But this is not the ongoing effect in those who have the Spirit of Christ. For them the effect is patient endurance, because the fruit of the Spirit is patience.

The point here is that until hardship comes into our lives, especially hardship for the sake of Christ and His righteousness, we do not experience the extent and depth of our devotion to Christ. Until times get hard, we do not taste and really know if we are fair-weather Christians – the kind Jesus described in the parable of the soils.

Mark 4:16-17 (NKJV) [16] These likewise are the ones sown on stony ground who, when they hear the word, immediately receive it with gladness; [17] and they have no root in themselves, and so endure only for a time. Afterward, when tribulation or persecution arises for the word's sake, immediately they stumble.

So Paul is saying that one great effect of tribulation is that it brings about patient endurance and perseverance in God's people, so they can see the faithfulness of God in their lives and know that they are truly His.

2. Proven Character

That's the point of the second effect that's mentioned (v. 4). "And [this] perseverance [brings about] proven character." Literally the word *dokimen* means "the experience of being tested and approved." We could say "approvedness" or "provenness."

This is not hard to grasp. If, when tribulations come, you persevere in devotion to Christ and don't turn against him, then you come out of that experience with a stronger sense that you are real, you are proven, you are not a hypocrite. The tree of trust was bent and it didn't break. Your fidelity and loyalty were put to the test and they passed. Now they have a "proven character." The gold of your faith was put in the fire and it came out refined, not consumed.

That's the second effect of affliction: the proving and refining of the gold of our allegiance to Jesus. Perseverance brings about the assurance of proveness.

3. Hope

The third effect comes from this sense of being tested and approved and refined. Verse 4b: "And proven character [brings about] hope." This takes us back to verse 2: "We exult in the hope of the glory of God." The Christian life begins with hope in the promises of God in the gospel, and it spirals up through affliction to more and more hope.

Approvedness brings about more hope because our hope grows when we experience the reality of our own authenticity through testing. The people who know God best are the people who suffer with Christ. The people who are most unwavering in their hope are those who have been tested most deeply. The people who look most earnestly and steadfastly and eagerly to the hope of glory are those who have had the comforts of this life stripped away through tribulations.

EXULTING IN THE HOPE OF GLORY AND IN TRIBULATION

So the first thing we say about suffering and affliction is that God has a purpose in it. And that purpose is to bring out the patient endurance of His people for the sake of His name; and through that to test and prove and refine the reality of faith and allegiance to Christ; and through that sense of approvedness to strengthen and deepen and intensify our hope.

We have ministry goals as a church (pastoral care, Christian education, discipleship, evangelism, leadership development); a missionary vision (Ukraine, Africa and other parts of the world); we have a building to pay, for a budget to fund for Christ and His kingdom. How much of this God in His sovereignty will bring to pass, I don't know. But this I know in our obedient pursuit of these goals God has a purpose for every obstacle and every frustration and every pain and every affliction, and that purpose is as important as the goals themselves – your perseverance, your proven character, and your hope in the glory of God.

Whatever else God may be doing at the planning level of our life; He is always developing and working at the heart level of your life. And so let us with Paul exult in the hope of glory and also in the tribulations that are coming.

CALLED TO SUFFER AND REJOICE: THAT WE MIGHT GAIN CHRIST

Philippians 3:1-14 (NKJV) [1] Finally, my brethren, rejoice in the Lord. For me to write the same things to you *is* not tedious, but for you *it is* safe. [2] Beware of dogs, beware of evil workers, beware of the mutilation! [3] For we are the circumcision, who worship God in the Spirit, rejoice in Christ Jesus, and have no confidence in the flesh, [4] though I also might have confidence in the flesh. If anyone else thinks he may have confidence in the flesh, I more so: [5] circumcised the eighth day, of the stock of Israel, *of* the tribe of Benjamin, a Hebrew of the Hebrews; concerning the law, a Pharisee; [6] concerning zeal, persecuting the church; concerning the righteousness which is in the law, blameless. [7] But what things were gain to me, these I have counted loss for Christ. [8] Yet indeed I also count all things loss for the excellence of the knowledge of Christ Jesus my Lord, for whom I have suffered the loss of all things, and count them as rubbish, that I may gain Christ [9] and be found in Him, not having my own righteousness, which *is* from the law, but that which *is* through faith in Christ, the righteousness which is from God by faith; [10] that I may know Him and the power of His resurrection, and the fellowship of His sufferings, being conformed to His death, [11] if, by any means, I may attain to the resurrection from the dead. [12] Not that I have already attained, or am already perfected; but I press on, that I may lay hold of that for which Christ Jesus has also laid hold of me. [13] Brethren, I do not count myself to have apprehended; but one thing *I do,* forgetting those things which are behind and reaching forward to those things which are ahead, [14] I press toward the goal for the prize of the upward call of God in Christ Jesus.

We have been focusing so far on the need to prepare for suffering. The reason for this is not just the fact that the days are evil and the path of righteousness costly, but the promise of the Bible that God's people will suffer.

For example, Acts 14:22 says that Paul told all his young churches, "Through many tribulations we must enter the kingdom." And Jesus said, "If they persecuted Me, they will persecute you" (John 15:20). And Peter said, "Do not be surprised at the fiery ordeal among you, which comes upon you for your testing, as though some strange thing were happening to you" (1 Peter 4:12). In other words it is not strange; it is to be expected. And Paul said (in 2 Timothy 3:12), "Indeed, all who desire to live godly in Christ Jesus will be persecuted."

So I take it to be a biblical truth that the more earnest we become about being the salt of the earth and the light of the world, and exposing the works of darkness, and loosing the bonds of sin and Satan, the more we will suffer. That's why we should prepare. And that is why I am including this section in building a foundation for our lives.

So far we have looked at the moral or spiritual purpose of suffering. That in suffering we come to hope more fully in God and put less confidence in the things of the world. The second area that we need to look at is the intimacy purpose: where we come to know Christ better when we share in His sufferings.

THE PURPOSE OF GREATER INTIMACY WITH CHRIST

God helps us prepare for suffering by teaching us and showing us that through suffering we are meant to go deeper in our relationship with Christ. You get to know Him better when you share His pain. The people who write most deeply and sweetly about the preciousness of Christ are people who have suffered with Him deeply.

For example, Jerry Bridges' book, *Trusting God, Even When Life Hurts*, is a deep and helpful book about suffering and going deep with God through affliction. And so it's not surprising to learn that when he was 14 years old, he heard his mother call out in the next room, totally unexpectedly, and arrived to see her take her last breath. He also has physical conditions that keep him from normal sports. And some years ago his wife died of cancer. Serving God with the Navigators has not spared him pain. He writes with depth about suffering because he has gone deep with Christ in suffering.

Over a hundred years ago Horatius Bonar, the Scottish pastor and hymn-writer, wrote a little book called Night of Weeping, or, "When God's Children Suffer." In it he said his goal was, "to minister to the saints . . . to seek to bear their burdens, to bind up their wounds, and to dry up at least some of their many tears." It is a tender and deep and wise book. So it's not surprising to hear him say,

"It is written by one who is seeking himself to profit by trial, and trembles lest it should pass by as the wind over the rock, leaving it as hard as ever; by one who would in every sorrow draw near to God that he may know Him more, and who is not unwilling to confess that as yet he knows but little."

Bridges and Bonar show us that suffering is a path deep into the heart of God. God has special revelations of his glory for his suffering children.

After months of suffering, Job finally says to God, "I had heard of thee by the hearing of the ear, but now my eye sees thee" (Job. 42:5). Job had been a godly and upright man, pleasing to God, but the difference between what he knew of God in prosperity and what he knew of him through adversity was the difference between hearing about and seeing.

When Stephen was arrested and put on trial for his faith and given a chance to preach, the upshot was that the religious leaders were enraged and ground their teeth at him. They were just about to drag him out of the city and kill him. At just that moment, Luke tells us, "Stephen was full of the Holy Spirit and gazed into heaven and saw the glory of God and Jesus standing at the right hand of God" (Acts 7:55). There is a special revelation, a special intimacy, prepared for those who suffer with Christ.

Peter put it this way, "If you are reproached for the name of Christ, you are blessed, because the Spirit of glory and of God rests upon you" (1 Peter 4:14). In other words God reserves a special coming and resting of His Spirit and His glory on His children who suffer for His name.

Focusing on this intimacy factor in suffering: one of the purposes of the saints is that their relationship with God might become less formal and less artificial and less distant, and become more personal and more real and more intimate, close and deep.

In out text (Philippians 3:5-11) we can make at least three observations:

1. First, Paul's preparation to suffer by reversing his values;
2. Second, Paul's experience of suffering and loss as the cost of his obedience to Christ;
3. Third, Paul's aim in all of this, namely, to gain Christ: to know Him and be in Him and fellowship with more intimacy and reality than he knew with his best friends Barnabas and Silas.

PAUL'S PREPARATION TO SUFFER

In verses 5 and 6 Paul lists the distinctives he enjoyed before he became a Christian. He gives his ethnic pedigree as a thoroughbred child of Abraham, a Hebrew of Hebrews This brought him great gain, a great sense of significance and assurance. He was an Israelite. Then he mentions three things that go right to the heart of Paul's life before he was a Christian (at the end of verse 5): "as to the law, a Pharisee; as to zeal, a persecutor of the church; as to the righteousness which is in the law, found blameless."

Paul's values Before He met Christ

This was Paul's life. This was what gave him meaning and significance. This was his gain, his fortune, his joy. Different strokes for different folks – and Paul's was that he belonged to the upper-echelon of law-keepers, the Pharisees, and that among them he was so zealous that he led the way in persecuting the enemies of God, the church of Jesus, and that he kept the law meticulously. He got strokes from belonging, he got strokes from excelling, he got strokes from God – or so he thought – for his blameless law-keeping.

And then he met Christ, the Son of God, on the Damascus road. Christ told him how much he would have to suffer (Acts 9:16). And Paul prepared himself.

Paul Counted His Prior Values as Loss

The way he prepared himself is described in verse 7. "But whatever things were gained to me, those things I have counted as loss for the sake of Christ." Paul looks at his standing in the upper-echelons of religious society, the Pharisees; he looks at the glory of being at the very top of that group with all its strokes and applause; he looks at the rigor of his law-keeping and the sense of moral pride he enjoyed; and he prepares to suffer by taking his whole world and turning it upside down, by reversing his values: "Whatever things were gain to me [that's verses 5-6], those things I have counted as loss."

Before he was a Christian he had a ledger with two columns: one that said, gains, and another that said, losses. On the gain side was the human glory of verses 5-6. On the loss side was the terrible prospect that this Jesus movement might get out of hand and Jesus prove real and win the day. When he met the living Christ on the Damascus road, Paul took a big red pencil and wrote "LOSS" in big red letters across his gains column that only had one name on it: Christ.

And not only that, the more Paul thought about the relative values of life in the world and the greatness of Christ, he moved beyond the few things mentioned in verses 5-6 and put everything but Christ in that first column: Verse 8: "More than that, I count all things to be loss in view of the surpassing value of knowing Christ Jesus my Lord." He started by counting his most precious accomplishments as loss, and he ended by counting everything as loss, except Christ.

Normal Christianity

That is what it meant for Paul to become a Christian. And lest anyone of us think he was unique or peculiar, notice that in verse 17 he says with his full apostolic authority, "Brethren, join in following my example." This is normal Christianity.

What Paul is doing here is showing how the teaching of Jesus is to be lived out. For example, Jesus said, "The kingdom of heaven is like a treasure hidden in a field, which a man found and hid; and from joy over it he goes and sells all that he has, and buys that field" (Matthew 14:44). Becoming a Christian means discovering that Christ (the King) is a Treasure Chest of holy joy and writing "LOSS" over everything else in the world in order to gain Him. "He sold all that he had to buy that field."

Or again in Luke 14:33 Jesus said, "No one of you can be my disciple who does not take leave of all his own possessions." In other words, becoming a disciple of Jesus means writing "LOSS" in big red letters over all your possessions – and everything else this world offers.

What Does This Mean Practically?

I think that it means four things. (1) It means that whenever I am called upon to choose between anything in this world and Christ, I choose Christ. (2) It means that I will deal with the things of this world in ways that draw me nearer to Christ so that I gain more of Christ and enjoy more of Him by the way I use the world. (3) It means that I will always deal with the things of this world in ways that show that they are not my treasure, but rather show that Christ is my treasure. (4) It means that if I lose any or all the things this world can offer I will not lose my joy or my treasure or my life, because Christ is all. Now this is what Paul reckoned in his soul (v. 8): "I count all things to be loss in view of the surpassing value of knowing Christ Jesus my Lord." Christ is all and all else is loss.

Why Is This a Way of Preparing to Suffer?

Now let's stand back a minute and get our bearings. I am still dealing with the first point: namely, that this is Paul's way of preparing to suffer. Why do I say that? Why is becoming a Christian, and writing "LOSS" across everything in your life but Christ a way of preparing to suffer?

The answer is that suffering is nothing more than the taking away of bad things or good things that the world offers for our enjoyment – reputation, esteem among peers, job, money, spouse, sexual life, children, friends, health, strength, sight, hearing, success, etc. When these things are taken away (by force or by circumstance or by choice), we suffer. But if we have followed Paul and the teaching of Jesus and have already counted them as loss for the surpassing value of gaining Christ, then we are prepared to suffer.

If when you become a Christian you write a big red "LOSS" across all the things in the world except Christ, then when Christ calls you to forfeit some of those things, it is not strange or unexpected. The pain and the sorrow may be great. The tears may be many, as they were for Jesus in Gethsemane. But we will be prepared. We will know that the value of Christ surpasses all the things the world can offer and that in losing them we gain more of Christ.

PAUL'S EXPERIENCE OF SUFFERING

So in the second half of verse 8 Paul moves from preparing for suffering to actual suffering. He moves from counting all things as loss in the first half of verse 8 to actually suffering the loss of all things in the second half of the verse. "...for whom [that is, Christ] I have suffered the loss of all things, and count them as rubbish in order that I might gain Christ." We are going to see this in the next section.

Paul had experienced so much actual loss of the normal benefits and comforts of the world that he could say that he was not merely counting things loss; he was suffering loss. He had prepared by turning his values upside down, and now he was being tested. Did he value Christ above all?

PAUL'S GOAL (AND GOD'S PURPOSE) IN SUFFERING

So let me close by riveting our attention on Paul's goal and God's purpose in this suffering. Why did God ordain and Paul accept the losses that it meant for him to be a Christian?

Paul gives the answer again and again in these verses so that we cannot miss the point. He is not passive in this suffering loss. He is purposeful. And his purpose is to gain Christ.

- Verse 7: "I count them loss for the sake of Christ."
- Verse 8a: "I count all things to be loss for the surpassing value of knowing Christ Jesus my Lord."
- Verse 8b: "For him I have suffered the loss of all things."
- Verse 8c: "And I count them but rubbish in order that I may gain Christ . . ."
- Verse 9: ". . . and that I may be found in Him [so as to have God's righteousness, not my own] . . "
- Verse 10a: (still giving his aim in accepting the loss of all things)" . . . that I may know Him."
- Verse 10b-11: (followed by four specifics of what it means to

know Christ)

- o "... [to know] the power of His resurrection"; and
- o "the fellowship of His sufferings";
- o "being conformed to His death";
- o "in order that I may attain to the resurrection from the dead."

In other words, what sustains Paul in suffering the loss of all things is the confidence that in his losing precious things in the world he is gaining something more precious – Christ.

And two times that gaining is called a knowing:

- Verse 8a: "... in view of the surpassing value of knowing Christ Jesus my Lord."
- Verse 10: "That I might know Him." This is the intimacy factor of suffering.

Do we want to know Him? Do we want to be more personal with Him and deep with Him and real with Him and intimate with Him – so much so that we count everything as loss to gain this greatest of all treasures?

If we do, we will be ready to suffer. If we don't, it will take us by surprise and we will rebel. May the Lord open our eyes to the surpassing worth of knowing Christ!

CALL TO SUFFER AND REJOICE: TO FINISH THE AIM OF CHRIST'S AFFLICTIONS

Colossians 1:24-29 (NKJV) [24] I now rejoice in my sufferings for you, and fill up in my flesh what is lacking in the afflictions of Christ, for the sake of His body, which is the church, [25] of which I became a minister according to the stewardship from God which was given to me for you, to fulfill the word of God, [26] the mystery which has been hidden from ages and from generations, but now has been revealed to His saints. [27] To them God willed to make known what are the riches of the glory of this mystery among the Gentiles: which is Christ in you, the hope of glory. [28] Him we preach, warning every man and teaching every man in all wisdom, that we may present every man perfect in Christ Jesus. [29] To this *end* I also labor, striving according to His working which works in me mightily.

Let's begin to focus on verse 24 and Paul's filling up that which is lacking in Christ's afflictions." How could anything be lacking in Christ's afflictions? Was not his suffering and death for us utterly all-sufficient? So what does he mean in verse 24 and how does it apply to us?

To see verse 24 properly let's look at it in connection with the rest of the verses. Starting at verse 29 let us go backward and sum up what Paul is saying in this paragraph.

Verse 29: Paul says that there is a purpose for which he labors. And the striving, the agonizing, of this labor is not merely his own energy. It is the power of Christ mightily working in him.

Verse 28 describes the purpose that Paul labors for, namely, to present everyone that he reaches "complete in Christ." And he does this by proclaiming Christ, admonishing everyone, and teaching everyone. This is Paul's ceaseless labor which Christ energizes.

Verse 26-27 defines more explicitly what Paul proclaims and teaches. It's called a "mystery" in verse 26, not because it can't be understood, but because it has been hidden for ages and has now been revealed to the saints. Then verse 27 describes the riches of the glory of this mystery. It is "Christ in you [Gentiles], the hope of glory." What was not revealed fully in past ages was that the Jewish Messiah – the Christ – would actually reach out to non-Jewish nations and indwell non-Jewish people – that He would actually live in them and give them the promise of Abraham, the hope of glory in the kingdom of God with all the saints.

But now the mystery is being revealed and Paul is proclaiming Christ and teaching everywhere that the indwelling of the Messiah and the hope of the glory of God belong to all who trust Christ and really hope in the glory of God (1:4, 23).

Verse 25 simply says that this proclamation of Christ is the fulfilling of a stewardship that God has given to Paul to spread God's Word. He is servant of the church and a steward of God. His charge is to take the Word of God to the nations, offer them the hope of glory, and call them to faith. And so he is a minister of the church by gathering God's chosen ones from among the nations, and by teaching and admonishing them so that they can be presented complete in Christ.

Verse 24 says that this ministry of extending the mystery of Christ and the hope of glory to the nations, and then admonishing and teaching them involves suffering. "Now I rejoice in my sufferings for your sake, and in my flesh I do my share on behalf of His body (which is the church) in filling up that which is lacking in Christ's afflictions."

WHAT DOES "FILL UP WHAT IS LACKING" MEAN?

Now what does this mean that when Paul suffers for the church – extending the hope of glory to more and more people, and teaching them about the mystery of Christ, and suffering in doing this – he is "filling up what is lacking in Christ's afflictions"? How can any man fill up what is surely as full as any suffering could be?

The Context Suggests the Meaning

I think the context that we just looked at suggests that Paul's sufferings fill up Christ's not by adding anything to their worth, but by extending them to the people they were meant to bless. What is lacking in the afflictions of Christ is not that they are deficient in worth or merit, as though they could not sufficiently cover the sins of all who believe. What is lacking is that the infinite value of Christ's afflictions are not known in the world. They are still a mystery (hidden) to most peoples. And God's intention is that the mystery be revealed, extended to all the Gentiles. So the afflictions are lacking in the sense that they are not seen and known among the nations. They must be carried by ministers of the Word. And those ministers of the Word fill up what is lacking in the afflictions of Christ by extending them to others.

Similar Words in Philippians 2:30

There is a strong confirmation of this in the use of similar words in Philippians 2:30. There was a man named Epaphroditus in the church at Philippi. When the church there gathered support for Paul (perhaps money or supplies or books), they decided to send them to Paul in Rome by the hand of Epaphroditus. In his travels with this supply Epaphroditus almost loses his life. Verse 27 says he was sick to the point of death, but God spared him.

Then in verse 29 Paul tells the church in Philippi to honor Epaphroditus when he comes back, and he gives his reason in verse 30 which has words very similar to Colossians 1:24.

"Because he came close to death for the work of Christ, risking his life to complete [i.e., fill up] what was deficient [i.e., lacking] in your service to me." Now in the original the phrase "completing what was deficient" in your service to me is almost the same as "filling up what is lacking" in Christ's afflictions in Colossians 1:24.

In what sense, then, was the service of the Philippians to Paul "lacking" and in what sense did Epaphroditus "fill up" what was lacking in their service? Over a hundred years ago a commentator, Marvin Vincent, I think gets it exactly right.

> "The gift to Paul was a gift of the church as a body. It was a sacrificial offering of love. What was lacking, and what would have been grateful to Paul and to the church alike, was the church's presentation of this offering in person. This was impossible, and Paul represents Epaphroditus as supplying this lack by his affectionate and zealous ministry. (*Epistle to the Philippians and to Philemon, ICC, p. 78*)"

HOW WE "FILL UP WHAT IS LACKING" IN CHRIST'S AFFLICTIONS

I think that is exactly what the words mean in Colossians 1:24 as well. Christ has prepared a love offering for the world by suffering and dying for sinners. It is full and lacking in nothing – except one thing, a personal presentation by Christ Himself to the nations of the world and the people of your workplace. God's answer to this lack is to call the people of Christ (people like Paul) to present the afflictions of Christ to the world – to carry them from Jerusalem to the ends of the earth.

In doing this we "fill up what is lacking in the afflictions of Christ." We finish what they were designed for, namely, a personal presentation to the world of people who do not know about their infinite worth.

But notice how Paul says this in verse 24: He says that it is in his suffering and in his flesh – that is, his actual, suffering body that he does his share in filling up the afflictions of Christ. Paul sees a very close connection between his sufferings and Christ's afflictions. What this means, I think, is that God intends for the afflictions of Christ to be presented to the world through the afflictions of his people. God really means for the body of Christ, the church, to experience some of the suffering He experienced so that when we offer the Christ of the cross to people, they see the Christ of the cross in us. We are to make the afflictions of Christ real for people by the afflictions we experience in offering Him to them, and living the life of love He lived.

"I rejoice in my sufferings for your sake . . . filling up that which is lacking in the afflictions of Christ." Christ wills to have a personal presentation of His sufferings to the world. And the way He means to offer Himself as a sufferer for the world to the world is through His people who, like Him, are willing to suffer for the world. His sufferings are completed in our sufferings because in ours the world sees His, and they have their appointed effect. The suffering love of Christ for sinners is seen in the suffering love of His people for sinners.

I think what we see in Colossians 1:24 is the living out of Jesus' words in Mark 8:35:

> **Mark 8:35** (NKJV) [35] For whoever desires to save his life will lose it, but whoever loses his life for My sake and the gospel's will save it.

The pathway of salvation Is the pathway of "losing one's life for the sake of the gospel." The point is that taking the gospel to people (across the office or across the ocean) ordinarily requires sacrifice and suffering, a losing of life or a denying of self. This is the way Christ means for His saving sufferings to be taken to the world, through the suffering of His people.

PAUL'S JOY IN THIS CALLING

Paul says that he rejoices in suffering. Verse 24: "Now I rejoice in my sufferings for your sake." The Calvary road is not a joyless road. It is a painful one, but it is a profoundly happy one. When we choose the fleeting pleasures of comfort and security over the sacrifices and sufferings of missions and evangelism and ministry and love, we choose against joy. We choose broken cisterns that can hold no water and reject the spring of water whose waters never fail (Isaiah 58:11).

The happiest people in the world are the people who know the mystery of Christ in them the hope of glory, satisfying their deep longings and freeing them to extend the sufferings of Christ through their own to the world.

God is calling us in this text to live for the sake of the gospel and to do that through suffering. Christ chose suffering, it just didn't happen to Him. He chose it as the way to create and perfect the church. Now He calls us to choose suffering. That is, He calls us to take up our cross and follow Him on the Calvery road and deny ourselves and make sacrifices for the sake of presenting His suffering to the world and ministering to the church.

I read a memorable way of saying this from the Romanian pastor and mission leader Joseph Tson. He said, "Christ's cross was for propitiation; ours is for propagation." That is, Christ suffered to accomplish salvation; we suffer to spread salvation. And our willingness to endure hardship for the good of others is a filling up of Christ's afflictions because it extends them to others and makes them visible.

THE STORY OF A MASAI WARRIOR NAMED JOSEPH

One of the least likely men to attend the Itinerant Evangelists' Conference in Amsterdam sponsored by the Billy Graham Association was a Masai Warrior named Joseph. But his story is told by Michael Card.

One day Joseph, who was walking along one of these hot, dirty African roads, met someone who shared the gospel of Jesus Christ with him. Then and there he accepted Jesus as his Lord and Savior. The power of the Spirit began transforming his life; he was filled with such excitement and joy that the first thing he wanted to do was return to his own village and share that same Good News with the members of his local tribe.

Joseph began going from door-to-door, telling everyone he met about the Cross [suffering!] of Jesus and the salvation it offered, expecting to see their faces light up the way his had. To his amazement the villagers not only didn't care, they became violent. The men of the village seized him and held him to the ground while the women beat him with strands of barbed wire. He was dragged from the village and left to die alone in the bush.

Joseph somehow managed to crawl to a water hole, and there, after days of passing in and out of consciousness, he found the strength to get up. He wondered about the hostile reception he had received from people he had known all his life. He decided he must have left something out or told the story of Jesus incorrectly. After rehearsing the message he had first heard, he decided to go back and share his faith once more.

Joseph limped into the circle of huts and began to proclaim Jesus. "He died for you, so that you might find forgiveness and come to know the living God" he pleaded. Again he was grabbed by the men of the village and held while the women beat him reopening wounds that had just begun to heal. Once more they dragged him unconscious from the village and left him to die.

To have suffered the first beating was truly remarkable. To live through the second was a miracle. Again, days later, Joseph awoke in the wilderness, bruised, scarred- and determined to go back.

He returned to the small village and this time, they attacked him before he had a chance to open his mouth. As they flogged him for the third and probably last time, he again spoke to them of Jesus Christ, the Lord. Before he passed out, the last thing he saw was that the women who were beating him began to weep.

This time he awoke in his own bed. The ones who had so severely beaten him were now trying to save his life and nurse him back to health. The entire village had come to Christ.

This is one vivid example of what Paul meant when he said, "I complete what is lacking in Christ's afflictions, for the sake of His body."

There is something profoundly freeing and stabilizing to know that Christ calls us to sacrifice for the sake of the gospel. It stabilizes us from being thrown off guard when it comes. And it frees us to choose it when love beckons us. And it begins to free us from the incredible seductions of American prosperity.

CALLED TO SUFFER AND REJOICE: FOR AN ETERNAL WEIGHT OF GLORY

> **2 Corinthians 4:7-8** (NKJV) [7] But we have this treasure in earthen vessels, that the excellence of the power may be of God and not of us. [8] We are hard-pressed on every side, yet not crushed; *we are* perplexed, but not in despair;

Verse 16 expresses something everyone who follows Christ wants to experience. Paul says, "We do not lose heart, but though our outer man is decaying, yet our inner man is being renewed day by day." There is something here nobody wants and something everybody wants.

WHAT NOBODY WANTS AND WHAT EVERYBODY WANTS

Nobody wants to lose heart. Nobody comes to church saying, "I sure hope we sing some songs and hear a sermon that helps me lose heart. I really want to be discouraged this morning by what the Pastor says." No, not one would say this. Nobody wants the heart for living knocked out of you. Neither did Paul.

On the contrary, everyone wants inner renewal day-by-day. We all know that feelings of strength and newness and hope and vitality and courage and zest for life last for a little while, and then they tend to drain away. If we are going to be strong on the inside and have hope and joy and resources to love, we are going to have to be renewed day by day. We know that life is not static or unfluctuating. It has its ups and downs. It is filled and depleted and filled again. It is renewed, expended, renewed and expended and renewed. And every one of us wants the power of renewal. Nobody wants to be left in the valley of depletion and emptiness and discouragement. If there is a secret to being made strong and hopeful and joyful and loving again and again day-by-day, we are interested.

TWO CRUCIAL WORDS: "THEREFORE" AND "FOR"

There are two words in this text that should get our attention; the word "therefore" at the beginning of verse 16 and the word "for" at the beginning of verse 17. Why are they so crucial?

Verse 16 as the Top of a Triangle

Picture verse 16 at the top of a triangle with two sides supporting it. So there is our longing supported by these two lines: "We do not lose heart . . . but our inner person is being renewed day by day." That's what we all want – to be able to say that and really mean it.

Verses 7-15 as One Side Supporting the Top

The word "therefore" at the front of the verse means that Paul has been saying some things that lead him to this experience and support it: "this is true and this is true and this is true" in verses 7-15, "THEREFORE we do not lose heart . . . THEREFORE we are being renewed day by day." So the first line of the triangle is the truth of verses 7-15 that leads up to this experience and supports it. That should get our attention and send us hunting in those verses for what it is. Maybe it is meant for us too!

Verses 17-18 as Another Side Supporting the Top

Then the word "for" at the beginning of the following verse (v. 17) means that Paul is about to say some things that are the reasons for verse 16. "We do not lose heart . . . and we are renewed day by day" FOR (BECAUSE) this is true and this is true and this is true. So the second line of the triangle coming down on the other side is the truth of verses 17-18 that support the experience he just described.

So can you see it now? The experience we long for is sitting there on the point of this triangle with two supporting sides. Verses 7-17 are true, "THEREFORE we do not lose heart but are renewed day by day." That's one side. "We do not lose heart, but are renewed day by day "FOR verses 17-18 are true.

So our aim then is to look at the two sides of this triangle and make the truth that sustained Paul the truth that sustains us.

VERSE 16 HAPPENS IN THE MIDST OF SUFFERING

But first, one brief observation: verse 16 acknowledges that not losing heart and being renewed day by day are happening in the midst of suffering. "We do not lost heart, but though our outer person is decaying our inner person is being renewed day by day." Paul knew that he was dying – and that everybody is dying. He experienced tremendous suffering, and in it he saw the decay and the wasting away of his earthly life. There were weaknesses and sicknesses and injuries and hardships and pressures and frustrations and disappointments. And every one of them cost him a piece of his life. One way to say it was "death was at work in him" (cf. v. 12).

That was the context for saying, "We do not lose heart . . . we are always being renewed." So what we are really asking now is not just, "How can I not lose heart in life?" and "How can I be renewed day-by-day?" but "How can I prepare to suffer without losing heart?" "How can I accept the decaying of my body and the ebbing away of my earthly life and at the same time not lose heart, but find renewed inner strength to go on with joy to the end with acts of love?"

Now we are ready to see Paul's answer to this question. First in verses 7-15 and then in verses 17-18.

VERSES 7-15: FOUR REASONS NOT TO LOSE HEART

In verses 7-15 there are at least four reasons that lead Paul to say < "THEREFORE, we do not lose heart." And every one of them takes into account the decaying of his earthly life. He never loses sight that he is a dying man and that his life is being spent. So what he is doing in these verses is to show what is true in spite of and even because his outer nature is decaying and wasting away.

1. The Glorification of God's Power and God's Son
First, though his outer nature is decaying, yet in and through this suffering, God's power and the life of God's Son are being manifested and glorified.

Verse 7: "WE have this treasure in earthen vessels [that Is, decaying, weak, outer persons], that the surpassing greatness of the power may be of God and not from ourselves." THEREFORE we do not lose heart . . . because God's power is exalted in our weakness.

Verse 10: "Always carrying about in the body the dying of Jesus [that's another aspect of the decaying of the outer man], that the life of Jesus also may be manifested in our body." THEREFORE we do not lose heart . . . because the life of God's Son is exalted in our daily dying.

Verse 11: "For we who live are constantly being delivered over to death for Jesus' sake, that the life of Jesus also may be manifested in our mortal flesh." THEREFORE we do not lose heart . . . because the life of God's Son is manifested and glorified in our decaying bodies.

So the first reason Paul doesn't lose heart, as his outer nature decays, is that in his weakness and his daily dying for the sake of others, God's power and the life of God's Son are glorified and that is what Paul loves more than anything.

2. The Strengthening of the Church
Second, though his outer nature is decaying, yet in and through this suffering life is flowing from him to the church. Christians are being strengthened by the fact that Paul is being weakened.

Verse 12: "So death is at work in us, but life in you." THEREFORE we do not lose heart . . . because not only is God being glorified, but you, my loved ones, are receiving life and strength and hope.

Verse 15: "For all things are for your sakes, that the grace which is spreading to more and more people [through Paul's suffering for them] may cause the giving of thanks to abound to the glory of God." THEREFORE we do not lose heart . . . because (and notice how verse 15 puts the first two reasons together) in my ministry of suffering grace is spreading to you and glory is going to God. These are the two great loves of Paul's life: bring grace to others and bring glory to God – and this verse says they happen in the very same experience. THEREFORE Paul does not lose heart.

3. God's Sustaining Presence
Third, though his outer nature is decaying, yet in and through this

suffering God sustains him and does not let him be overcome.

Verses 8-9 (notice in each of these pairs what he is really saying is: Yes, our outer nature is decaying, but, No, we do not lost heart): "We are afflicted in every way, but not crushed; perplexed, but not despairing; persecuted, but not forsaken; struck down, but not destroyed." THEREFORE we do not lose heart . . . because God sustains us and does not let us be overcome.

4. Our Resurrection from the Dead

Fourth, though his outer nature is decaying, yet he will be raised from the dead with the church and be with Jesus.

Verse 14: "[We know] that he who raised the Lord Jesus will raise us also with Jesus and will present is with you." THEREFORE we do not lose heart . . . because it's going to be all right. Not even death can make the story have a bad ending. I'm going to live again; and I am going to live with you, the people I love; and I am going to live with Jesus and share His glory forever and ever.

THEREFORE . . . That's the first line of the triangle (verses 7-15) that supports the great experience of not losing heart but being renewed every day.

1. I am renewed because God's power and the life of God's Son are being manifested and glorified in my decaying weakness.
2. I am being renewed because life is flowing from my suffering into the church that I love so much.
3. I am being renewed because God sustains me in my suffering and does not let me be overcome by it.
4. I am being renewed because I know I will be raised from the dead with you and with Jesus to live together forever and ever. THEREFORE I do not lose heart!

VERSES 17-18: FOUR REASONS NOT TO LOSE HEART

Now look at the other line of the triangle that supports Paul's wonderful experience in verse 16, namely, verses 17-18. He does not lose heart, and he is being renewed day by day FOR verses 17-18 are true. Again there are four reasons for Paul's not losing heart in spite of his decaying outer man – his weaknesses and sicknesses and injuries and hardships.

1. Momentary Affliction

He does not lost heart FOR his affliction is momentary.

Verse 17: "For momentary light affliction . . . " This does not mean it lasts 60 seconds. It means it only lasts a lifetime (which is momentary compared with a million ages of millenniums) and that's all. The word means "present" – "The present afflictions" – the afflictions that will not outlive this present life. I do not lose heart . . . FOR my afflictions will end. They will not have the last say in my life.

2. Light Affliction

He does not lose heart FOR his affliction is light.

Verse 17: "For momentary light affliction . . . "This is not the judgment of a comfortable modern American. This is Paul's own judgment. Nor had Paul forgotten what he says in 2 Corinthians 11:23-27.

> **2 Corinthians 11:23-27** (NKJV) [23] Are they ministers of Christ?—I speak as a fool—I *am* more: in labors more abundant, in stripes above measure, in prisons more frequently, in deaths often. [24] From the Jews five times I received forty *stripes* minus one. [25] Three times I was beaten with rods; once I was stoned; three times I was shipwrecked; a night and a day I have been in the deep; [26] in journeys often, *in* perils of waters, *in* perils of robbers, *in* perils of *my own* countrymen, *in* perils of the Gentiles, *in* perils in the city, *in* perils in the wilderness, *in* perils in the sea, *in* perils among false brethren; [27] in weariness and toil, in sleeplessness often, in hunger and thirst, in fastings often, in cold and nakedness—

When Paul says his afflictions are light, he does not mean easy or painless. He means that compared to what is coming they are as nothing. Compared to the weight of glory coming, they are like feathers in the scale. "I consider that the sufferings of this present time are not worthy to be compared to the glory to be revealed to us" (Romans 8:18. I do not lose heart . . . FOR my afflictions are light.

3.   An Eternal Weight of Glory

He does not lose heart FOR his affliction is actually producing for Paul an eternal weight of glory far beyond all comparison.

Verse 17: "For momentary, light affliction is producing for us an eternal weight of glory far beyond all comparison." What is coming to Paul is not momentary, but eternal. It is not light, but weighty. It's not affliction, but glory. And it is beyond all comprehension. Eye has not seen nor ear heard what God has prepared for those who love Him (1 Corinthians 2:9).

And the point is not that the afflictions merely precede the glory; they help produce the glory. There is a real causal connection between how we endure hardship now and how much we will be able to enjoy the glory of God in the ages to come. Not one moment of patient pain is wasted. I do not lose heart . . . FOR all my troubles are producing for me an eternal weight of glory beyond all comparison.

4.   The Unseen, Eternal Glory to Come

Paul does not lose heart FOR he sets his mind on the unseen, eternal glory to come.

Verse 18: "We look not at the things which are seen, but at the things which are not seen." God might offer you all the glory in the universe to keep you from losing heart and to renew your soul day by day, but if you never looked at it, nothing would come of it.

GOD'S LAVISH INVITATION

In fact that is what God is doing right now. This text is one lavish invitation from God for you to look at all the reasons why you don't have to lose heart – all the reasons why you can be renewed day by day.

- Look! The power of God and the life of His Son are manifested in your weakness.
- Look! The life of Jesus is flowing through your suffering into the lives of other people.
- Look! God sustains you in your afflictions and will not let you be destroyed.
- Look! Your afflictions will not have the last word; you will rise from the dead with Jesus and with the church of God and live in joy forever and ever.
- Look! Your afflictions are momentary. They are only for now, not for the age to come.
- Look! Your afflictions are light. Compared to the pleasures of what is coming they are as nothing.
- Look! These afflictions are producing for you an eternal weight of glory beyond all comparison.

So LOOK! Focus! Meditate! Think on these things! Believe what God says. And you will not lose heart, but your inner person will be renewed day by day.

CHAPTER 10

LAYING ON OF HANDS

The doctrine of the laying on of hands is the fourth of the "first principles" which form "the foundation" of the Christian life.

The doctrine of the laying on of hands is a natural progression from the first three fundamental truths of Hebrews 6:1: repentance, faith, and baptism. The first three elements are inward-directed parts of our faith, but the laying on of hands is an outward-directed element that enables us to be instruments of Christ's blessing.

Laying on of hands occurs a number of times in the Bible, and we shall consider most of these. However, as an elementary Christian doctrine, it specifically refers to the reception of the Holy Spirit. The act of laying on of hands, signifies "transference, transmission, impartation, and identification."

LAYING ON OF HANDS IN THE OLD TESTAMENT

Jacob laid his hands on his grandchildren and blessed them (Genesis 48:13-20). This is the first occurrence of the laying on of hands for the purpose of symbolizing the transmission of spiritual benefit. With his hands laid on the heads of Ephraim and Manasseh, Jacob prayed, "The Angel which redeemed me from all evils, bless the lads!" Thus, in this first instance of the laying on of hands, we are taught something of its symbolic meaning. When Jacob put his hand upon Ephraim, it displeased Joseph because Manasseh was his firstborn. By switching the blessing, Jacob was said to have "put Ephraim ahead of Manasseh." Through the laying on of Jacob's right hand, Ephraim received the first and greater blessing. Then through the laying on of Jacob's left hand, Manasseh received the lesser blessing, though a blessing nevertheless.

The Israelite and his sacrificial offering (Lev. 1:4; 3:2; 16:21). God required the Israelite to bring an animal sacrifice to the "door of the Tabernacle which was directly in front of the Brazen Altar." Before the sacrificial animal was slain and offered, the Israelite was required to "put his hand upon the head of the burnt offering", with the accompanying promise that it "shall be accepted for him to make atonement for him."

In putting his hand on the head of the sacrificial animal, the Israelite was indicating the transference of his sin and guilt to the victim, and by this symbolic act implying, "This animal is now myself, and its life is my life."

As Jacob's act symbolized the transmission of blessing, the Israelite act symbolized the transmission or transference of sin and guilt.

This is further seen in the sacrificial ceremony on the Day of Atonement. On this great day of national contrition, Aaron, the High Priest, representing the people, "shall lay both his hands upon the head of the live goat, and confess over him all the iniquities of the children of Israel, and all their transgressions in all their sins, putting them upon the head of the goat…" Here transmission and transference are clearly symbolized.

The children of Israel and the Levites (Numbers 8:10). The Levites were ordained by God to "service the tabernacle of meeting" (vs. 15). In this service they represented the congregation. The "laying on of hands signified service of the sanctuary was transferred from the whole congregation to the Levites." So, again, we see the principle of transference and identification symbolized in the laying on of hands.

Moses and Joshua (Numbers 27:15-23; Deuteronomy 34:9). In appointing a successor to Moses, God instructed the great leader to "Take Joshua and lay thine hand upon him." In so doing, God said, "thou shalt put some of thine honour upon him." That there was also at that time an impartation of spiritual enablement, is indicated in the Deuteronomy passage, which says that "Joshua, the son of Nun, was full of the Holy Spirit of wisdom: for Moses had laid his hands upon him."

So we see in the Old Testament the laying on of hands was practiced for the following reasons:

1. The impartation of blessing.

2. The setting in place of leaders. The public acknowledgment of them as leaders over the people.

3. The anointing of leaders for service. The impartation of authority and wisdom to lead.

4. In the Levitical sacrifice, the laying on of hands symbolized substitution and the transfer of punishment. Again, the idea of impartation is present.

THE LAYING ON OF HANDS IN THE NEW TESTAMENT

In the New Testament, there are seven distinct purposes for which the laying on of hands is used:

1. To impart blessing and strength.

Matthew 19:13-15 (NKJV) [13] Then little children were brought to Him that He might put *His* hands on them and pray, but the disciples rebuked them. [14] But Jesus said, "Let the little children come to Me, and do not forbid them; for of such is the kingdom of heaven " [15] And He laid *His* hands on them and departed from there.

Mark 10:13-16 (NKJV) [13] Then they brought little children to Him, that He might touch them; but the disciples rebuked those who brought *them*. [14] But when Jesus saw *it*, He was greatly displeased and said to them, "Let the little children come to Me, and do not forbid them; for of such is the kingdom of God. [15] Assuredly, I say to you, whoever does not receive the kingdom of God as a little child will by no means enter it." [16] And He took them up in His arms, laid *His* hands on them, and blessed them.

These parents knew the power for blessing that the Lord Jesus possessed. They also knew that it could be imparted to them and their children through the laying on of His hands.

Jesus put His hand on John and said, "Do not be afraid" (Rev. 1:17).

2. **The ministry of healing.**

> **Mark 16:17-18** (NKJV) [17] And these signs will follow those who believe: In My name they will cast out demons; they will speak with new tongues; [18] they will take up serpents; and if they drink anything deadly, it will by no means hurt them; they will lay hands on the sick, and they will recover."

Through the laying on of hands by believers, supernatural healing can be ministered to the sick. Please notice that Jesus did not say the sick would be healed instantaneously. He simply promised, "they will get well," leaving the question of timing open. Sometimes healing is received immediately; other times the healing comes as a gradual process. Nonetheless, the promise is sure, and we should stand on it: "they will get well."

Furthermore, the ministry of healing through the laying on of hands was not just given to the apostles or to the early church, but it was given to "those who believe." All believers have this authority in the Lord Jesus Christ!

Jesus had this power:

> **Matthew 8:3** (NKJV) [3] Then Jesus put out *His* hand and touched

him, saying, "I am willing; be cleansed." Immediately his leprosy was cleansed.

Mark 6:5 (NKJV) [5] Now He could do no mighty work there, except that He laid His hands on a few sick people and healed *them.*

This verse in Mark 6 tells us that the few who were healed in Nazareth were healed through the laying on of hands, thereby suggesting that the laying on of hands will work when nothing else will!

Matthew 8:15 (NKJV) [15] So He touched her hand, and the fever left her. And she arose and served them.

Mark 8:22-25 (NKJV) [22] Then He came to Bethsaida; and they brought a blind man to Him, and begged Him to touch him. [23] So He took the blind man by the hand and led him out of the town. And when He had spit on his eyes and put His hands on him, He asked him if he saw anything. [24] And he looked up and said, "I see men like trees, walking." [25] Then He put *His* hands on his eyes again and made him look up. And he was restored and saw everyone clearly.

Mark 7:32 (NKJV) [32] Then they brought to Him one who was deaf and had an impediment in his speech, and they begged Him to put His hand on him.

Mark 5:22-23 (NKJV) [22] And behold, one of the rulers of the synagogue came, Jairus by name. And when he saw Him, he fell at His feet [23] and begged Him earnestly, saying, "My little daughter lies at the point of death. Come and lay Your hands on her, that she may be healed, and she will live."

The early church ministered healing through the laying on of hands:

Acts 5:12 (NKJV) [12] And through the hands of the apostles many signs and wonders were done among the people. And they were all with one accord in Solomon's Porch.

Acts 19:11-12 (NKJV) [11] Now God worked unusual miracles by the hands of Paul, [12] so that even handkerchiefs or aprons were brought from his body to the sick, and the diseases left them and the evil spirits went out of them.

Acts 28:8-9 (NKJV) [8] And it happened that the father of Publius lay sick of a fever and dysentery. Paul went in to him and prayed, and he laid his hands on him and healed him. [9] So when this was done, the rest of those on the island who had diseases also came and were healed.

Elders are told to anoint with oil (by their hands) and pray for others' healing.

James 5:14-16 (NKJV) [14] Is anyone among you sick? Let him call for the elders of the church, and let them pray over him, anointing him with oil in the name of the Lord. [15] And the prayer of faith will save the sick, and the Lord will raise him up. And if he has committed sins, he will be forgiven. [16] Confess *your* trespasses to one another, and pray for one another, that you may be healed. The effective, fervent prayer of a righteous man avails much.

Believers are instructed to impart healing by the power of the laying on of hands. And in Jesus' name we have this power (Mark 16:17-18; Acts 9:17; 28:8-9).

3.   **To receive the infilling in the Holy Spirit**

We can receive the infilling of the Holy Spirit in several ways:

- Simply by asking the Father to fill us with His Spirit.

Luke 11:13 (NKJV) [13] If you then, being evil, know how to give good gifts to your children, how much more will *your* heavenly Father give the Holy Spirit to those who ask Him!"

- In a spontaneous, sovereign outpouring from God.

Acts 2:2-4 (NKJV) [2] And suddenly there came a sound from heaven, as of a rushing mighty wind, and it filled the whole house where they were sitting. [3] Then there appeared to them divided tongues, as of fire, and *one* sat upon each of them. [4] And they were all filled with the Holy Spirit and began to speak with other tongues, as the Spirit gave them utterance.

Acts 10:44 (NKJV) [44] While Peter was still speaking these words, the Holy Spirit fell upon all those who heard the word.

- Through the laying on of hands.

Acts 9:10 (NKJV) [10] Now there was a certain disciple at Damascus named Ananias; and to him the Lord said in a vision, "Ananias." And he said, "Here I am, Lord."

Acts 8:18 (NKJV) [18] And when Simon saw that through the laying on of the apostles' hands the Holy Spirit was given, he offered them money,

Acts 9:17 (NKJV) [17] And Ananias went his way and entered the house; and laying his hands on him he said, "Brother Saul, the Lord Jesus, who appeared to you on the road as you came, has sent me that you may receive your sight and be filled with the Holy Spirit."

Acts 19:6 (NKJV) [6] And when Paul had laid hands on them, the Holy Spirit came upon them, and they spoke with tongues and prophesied.

4. **To impart spiritual gifts.**

1 Timothy 4:14 (NKJV) [14] Do not neglect the gift that is in you, which was given to you by prophecy with the laying on of the hands of the eldership.

2 Timothy 1:6 (NKJV) [6] Therefore I remind you to stir up the gift of God which is in you through the laying on of my hands.

Romans 1:11 (NKJV) [11] For I long to see you, that I may impart to you some spiritual gift, so that you may be established—

5. **To commission ministries.**

   Acts 13:1-4 (NKJV) [1] Now in the church that was at Antioch there were certain prophets and teachers: Barnabas, Simeon who was called Niger, Lucius of Cyrene, Manaen who had been brought up with Herod the tetrarch, and Saul. [2] As they ministered to the Lord and fasted, the Holy Spirit said, "Now separate to Me Barnabas and Saul for the work to which I have called them." [3] Then, having fasted and prayed, and laid hands on them, they sent *them* away. [4] So, being sent out by the Holy Spirit, they went down to Seleucia, and from there they sailed to Cyprus.

6. **To appoint elders in the local church.**

   1 Timothy 5:22 (NKJV) [22] Do not lay hands on anyone hastily, nor share in other people's sins; keep yourself pure.

7. **To appoint men for specific acts of service in the church.**

   Acts 6:3-6 (NKJV) [3] Therefore, brethren, seek out from among you seven men of *good* reputation, full of the Holy Spirit and wisdom, whom we may appoint over this business; [4] but we will give ourselves continually to prayer and to the ministry of the word." [5] And the saying pleased the whole multitude. And they chose Stephen, a man full of faith and the Holy Spirit, and Philip, Prochorus, Nicanor, Timon, Parmenas, and Nicolas, a proselyte from Antioch, [6] whom they set before the apostles; and when they had prayed, they laid hands on them.

CARE SHOULD BE TAKEN IN THE LAYING ON OF HANDS (1 TIMOTHY 5:22)

One brother speaks about people laying "empty hands on empty heads." He knew of a woman who went to a meeting where hands were laid on her. She was then prophesied over and supposedly was given "the gift of casting out permanent waves." He told her if she could have gotten the gift of putting them in, she would have had something.

There are two kinds of "unprofitable" laying on of hands:

1. **Mere ritual.**

Some churches have the ritual of laying on of hands to "confirm" people. According to their creeds the Holy Spirit is given at this time. However, this is mere tradition and formality, and nothing necessarily happens. Also, men can be set in leadership positions with hands laid on them. But again, if it is only done as a tradition with no faith present, nothing will be imparted.

In the examples we looked at from both testaments, it is clear that in the Bible the laying on of hands was no mere ritual; it definitely accomplished things.

2. **Extremes in Pentecostal and Charismatic circles.**

In some Spirit-filled churches, people have hands laid on them for nearly anything with nothing being accomplished. There are many people who have had hands laid on them, often with accompanying glorious prophecies of imparted giftings and ministries, and yet, in reality, the people received nothing.

Let us avoid the abuses and excesses, but let us not draw back from the

New Testament practices of the laying on of hands.

METHODS OF LAYING ON OF HANDS

The laying on of hands can be done in two ways:

1. Any believer can lay hands upon a fellow believer as a point of contact to release faith and expect that person to be healed (Mark 16:17-18).

2. Laying on of hands is used as a means of serving. The basic Christian ministry is service (Mark 10:43-45). Using your hands to serve can be one method to express your love and concern to others in the body of Christ and to the world. Imparting blessing or healing by the laying on of hands can be one of the greatest acts of service you can do for another human being. When you lay hands on others by faith, you minister or give the life of God within you to them.

3. Laying on of hands enables the call in the lives of believers. The church of Jesus Christ needs men and women with a call from God and the gifting or anointing, to enable them to carry out that call. The laying on of hands by anointed leadership in the body of Christ is one way of imparting such enabling to those whom God calls (Acts 13:1-3).

SUMMARY

The laying on of hands draws life from Jesus, the Head of the body of Christ, and releases and imparts that life via the hands. The power of the risen Christ to heal, to minister, or to give blessing is resident in the life of every Spirit-filled disciple, but especially in God-chosen leaders. That power is released through the laying on of hands.

CHAPTER 11

RESURRECTION OF THE DEAD

"Resurrection of the dead" is the fifth of the six principles referred to as "foundational" in Hebrews 6. A commitment in heart and mind to the revelation of the Word of God concerning "resurrection" is essential to a sound foundation. Error or weakness here, will affect the whole structure of Christian life. It is faith in a resurrected Christ that gives meaning to certain hope of the resurrection of our own bodies in the future. In fact, Paul says "no resurrection...no faith" (1 Corinthians 15:13, 14).

We shall consider this subject under four main headings:

1. Resurrection was foretold in the Old and New Testaments.

2. Jesus' resurrection.

3. The resurrection of men.

4. The nature of the resurrection.

RESURRECTION FORETOLD IN THE OLD AND NEW TESTAMENTS

JESUS' RESURRECTION WAS A FULFILLMENT OF OLD TESTAMENT PROPHECIES.

> **1 Corinthians 15:4** (NKJV) [4] and that He was buried, and that He rose again the third day according to the Scriptures,

The "Scriptures" that Paul speaks of here are the Old Testament Scriptures. For example, Jesus' resurrection was specifically predicted in

Psalm 16:

> **Psalm 16:8-11** (NKJV) [8] I have set the LORD always before me; Because *He is* at my right hand I shall not be moved. [9] Therefore my heart is glad, and my glory rejoices; My flesh also will rest in hope. [10] For You will not leave my soul in Sheol, Nor will You allow Your Holy One to see corruption. [11] You will show me the path of life; In Your presence *is* fullness of joy; At Your right hand *are* pleasures forevermore.

On the Day of Pentecost, Peter quoted these same verses and applied them to Jesus' death, burial, resurrection and ascension:

> **Acts 2:25-31** (NKJV) [25] For David says concerning Him: 'I foresaw the LORD always before my face, *For He is at my right hand, that I may not be shaken.* [26] *Therefore my heart rejoiced, and my tongue was glad;* Moreover my flesh also will rest in hope. [27] *For You will not leave my soul in Hades,* Nor will You allow Your Holy One to see corruption. [28] *You have made known to me the ways of life;* You will make me full of joy in Your presence.' [29] "Men *and* brethren, let *me* speak freely to you of the patriarch David, that he is both dead and buried, and his tomb is with us to this day. [30] Therefore, being a prophet, and knowing that God had sworn with an oath to him that of the fruit of his body, according to the flesh, He would raise up the Christ to sit on his throne, [31] he, foreseeing this, spoke concerning the resurrection of the Christ, that His soul was not left in Hades, nor did His flesh see corruption.

Bodily resurrection in general was predicted in the Old Testament.

> **Job 19:25-27** (NKJV) [25] For I know *that* my Redeemer lives, And He shall stand at last on the earth; [26] And after my skin is destroyed,

this *I know,* That in my flesh I shall see God, [27] Whom I shall see for myself, And my eyes shall behold, and not another. *How* my heart yearns within me!

In this beautiful Scripture, Job said that even though his body would die and decompose, he knew that in his "flesh" (i.e. his resurrected body) he would "see God." This is clear prophetic anticipation of the resurrection of the Last Day.

> **Isaiah 26:19** (NKJV) [19] Your dead shall live; *Together with* my dead body they shall arise. Awake and sing, you who dwell in dust; For your dew *is like* the dew of herbs, And the earth shall cast out the dead.

Isaiah spoke of his own bodily resurrection along with the resurrection of all the righteous dead from the "dust." His image of "dew" is probably a prophetic reference to the supernatural power of the Holy Spirit that will come like moisture to dry seeds that lie buried in the dust, making them germinate and spring up.

> **Daniel 12:1-2** (NKJV) [1] "At that time Michael shall stand up, The great prince who stands *watch* over the sons of your people; And there shall be a time of trouble, Such as never was since there was a nation, *Even* to that time. And at that time your people shall be delivered, Every one who is found written in the book. [2] And many of those who sleep in the dust of the earth shall awake, Some to everlasting life, Some to shame *and* everlasting contempt.

The first part of this prophecy refers to the time of "Great Tribulation" on the earth. Daniel says "at that time…Multitudes who sleep in the dust of the earth will awake." This is clear prophecy of the bodily resurrection of both the righteous and the wicked.

Furthermore, Daniel was personally told by the angels who spoke with him:

Daniel 12:13 (NKJV) [13] "But you, go *your way* till the end; for you shall rest, and will arise to your inheritance at the end of the days.

The word "rise" refers to Daniel's own bodily resurrection "at the end of the days."

Hosea 6:1-3 (NKJV) [1] Come, and let us return to the LORD; For He has torn, but He will heal us; He has stricken, but He will bind us up. [2] After two days He will revive us; On the third day He will raise us up, That we may live in His sight. [3] Let us know, Let us pursue the knowledge of the LORD. His going forth is established as the morning; He will come to us like the rain, Like the latter *and* former rain to the earth.

In Corinthians 15:4, Paul said that Jesus "was raised on the third day according to the Scriptures." Here in Hosea, is a Scripture that specifically predicted Jesus' resurrection "on the third day." Hosea's prophecy was addressed to the spiritual resurrection of national Israel as well as to the bodily resurrection of all believers. All the saved will be resurrected in union with Jesus' resurrection.

Ephesians 2:4-6 (NKJV) [4] But God, who is rich in mercy, because of His great love with which He loved us, [5] even when we were dead in trespasses, made us alive together with Christ (by grace you have been saved), [6] and raised *us* up together, and made *us* sit together in the heavenly *places* in Christ Jesus,

In that sense, we are resurrected "on the third day" when Jesus was resurrected. Thus, this prophecy predicts our future bodily resurrection as well as Jesus' resurrection on the third day.

Another Old Testament prophecy regarding the "third day" is found in the Book of Jonah. Jonah was inside the fish for three days and nights (Jonah 1:17), and Jesus said Jonah's experience was a type of His body being in the tomb for three days and nights (Matthew 12:38-40; John 2:18-22) before His resurrection.

Bodily resurrection was typified in the Old Testament when Elijah and Elisha raised the dead (1 Kings 17; 2 Kings 4).

Furthermore, both Enoch and Elijah were translated from earth to heaven in a wonderful picture of the coming resurrection of the righteous.

Jesus predicted His own resurrection.

> **Matthew 20:19** (NKJV) [19] and deliver Him to the Gentiles to mock and to scourge and to crucify. And the third day He will rise again."

> **John 2:19-22** (NKJV) [19] Jesus answered and said to them, "Destroy this temple, and in three days I will raise it up." [20] Then the Jews said, "It has taken forty-six years to build this temple, and will You raise it up in three days?" [21] But He was speaking of the temple of His body. [22] Therefore, when He had risen from the dead, His disciples remembered that He had said this to them; and they believed the Scripture and the word which Jesus had said. [cf. Matt. 16:21; 17:22-23; Luke 9:22; 18:31-34]

The resurrection of the dead was predicted in the New Testament.

By Jesus:

> **John 5:28-29** (NKJV) [28] Do not marvel at this; for the hour is coming in which all who are in the graves will hear His voice [29] and come forth— those who have done good, to the resurrection of life, and those who have done evil, to the resurrection of condemnation.

By Paul:

1 Corinthians 15:21-23 (NKJV) [21] For since by man *came* death, by Man also *came* the resurrection of the dead. [22] For as in Adam all die, even so in Christ all shall be made alive. [23] But each one in his own order: Christ the firstfruits, afterward those *who are* Christ's at His coming. [cf. vv. 35-54]

By John:

Revelation 20:5 (NKJV) [5] But the rest of the dead did not live again until the thousand years were finished. This *is* the first resurrection. [cf. vv. 12-13]

Bodily resurrection was typified in the New Testament when Jesus raised the dead.

Matthew 9:18-25 (NKJV) [18] While He spoke these things to them, behold, a ruler came and worshiped Him, saying, "My daughter has just died, but come and lay Your hand on her and she will live." [19] So Jesus arose and followed him, and so *did* His disciples. [20] And suddenly, a woman who had a flow of blood for twelve years came from behind and touched the hem of His garment. [21] For she said to herself, "If only I may touch His garment, I shall be made well." [22] But Jesus turned around, and when He saw her He said, "Be of good cheer, daughter; your faith has made you well." And the woman was made well from that hour. [23] When Jesus came into the ruler's house, and saw the flute players and the noisy crowd wailing, [24] He said to them, "Make room, for the girl is not dead, but sleeping." And they ridiculed Him. [25] But when the crowd was put outside, He went in and took her by the hand, and the girl arose.

Luke 7:11-15 (NKJV) [11] Now it happened, the day after, *that* He went into a city called Nain; and many of His disciples went with Him, and a large crowd. [12] And when He came near the gate of the city, behold, a dead man was being carried out, the only son of his mother; and she was a widow. And a large crowd from the city was with her. [13] When the Lord saw her, He had compassion on her and said to her, "Do not weep." [14] Then He came and touched the open coffin, and those who carried *him* stood still. And He said, "Young man, I say to you, arise." [15] So he who was dead sat up and began to speak. And He presented him to his mother.

John 11:43-44 (NKJV) [43] Now when He had said these things, He cried with a loud voice, "Lazarus, come forth!" [44] And he who had died came out bound hand and foot with graveclothes, and his face was wrapped with a cloth. Jesus said to them, "Loose him, and let him go."

JESUS' RESURRECTION

The Gospel does not tell only of the death of Jesus, but also of His resurrection:

1 Corinthians 15:1-4 (NKJV) [1] Moreover, brethren, I declare to you the gospel which I preached to you, which also you received and in which you stand, [2] by which also you are saved, if you hold fast that word which I preached to you—unless you believed in vain. [3] For I delivered to you first of all that which I also received: that Christ died for our sins according to the Scriptures, [4] and that He was buried, and that He rose again the third day according to the Scriptures,

The resurrection of Jesus is mentioned over 100 times in the New Testament. The preaching of the resurrection was the cause of the first persecution of the church (Acts 4:1-3; 5:27-42). The resurrection of Jesus is the foundation of Christianity:

Romans 10:9 (NKJV) [9] that if you confess with your mouth the Lord Jesus and believe in your heart that God has raised Him from the dead, you will be saved.

The resurrection of Jesus was the evidence that the atonement was complete and had been accepted by God. We're redeemed by the precious blood of Jesus and not by His resurrection, but His resurrection proved that He paid the penalty for sin fully or else He wouldn't have been raised. It is in this sense that Paul wrote in Romans 4:25 that Jesus was "raised to life for our justification."

Romans 4:25 (NKJV) [25] who was delivered up because of our offenses, and was raised because of our justification.

1 Peter 1:3 (NKJV) [3] Blessed *be* the God and Father of our Lord Jesus Christ, who according to His abundant mercy has begotten us again to a living hope through the resurrection of Jesus Christ from the dead,

WE SHALL NOW CONSIDER SOME FACTS CONCERNING JESUS' RESURRECTION.

Jesus' body saw no decay.

Acts 13:35 (NKJV) [35] Therefore He also says in another *Psalm:* 'You will not allow Your Holy One to see corruption.'

In this Scripture, Paul said that Jesus' holy body did not see decay. Decay speaks of physical decomposition and corruption. It is part of the curse of sin and the common lot of fallen humanity (Genesis 3:19; Psalm 49:9). Jesus, however, was sinless; therefore, His body could not experience decay while it was in the tomb.

In Acts 13:35-37, Paul makes a contrast between the body of David (an imperfect man) and the body of Jesus (God's Holy One). David's body saw decay while Jesus' body saw no decay.

If Jesus' body had experienced decay, it would mean that He had been tainted by sin when He died, and therefore, He could not have been an acceptable sacrifice to God for our sins (Leviticus 22:20). If Christ was not raised from the dead without seeing decay, then no atonement was made and we are still in our sins. However, by virtue of His absolute sinlessness, Jesus' body was incorruptible (1 Peter 1:18-19); therefore, Paul continues with the promise of forgiveness of sins and salvation through Him.

> **Acts 13:38-39** (NKJV) [38] Therefore let it be known to you, brethren, that through this Man is preached to you the forgiveness of sins; [39] and by Him everyone who believes is justified from all things from which you could not be justified by the law of Moses.

Jesus could not have stayed dead.

> **Acts 2:24** (NKJV) [24] whom God raised up, having loosed the pains of death, because it was not possible that He should be held by it.

In Acts 2:24, Peter says that it was "impossible" for Jesus to be held by death. In other words, Jesus could not have stayed physically dead. Jesus paid the full price for man's sins when He shed His precious blood on the cross; therefore, once He had died, there was no more penalty to be borne by Him in our place.

Jesus was sinless, and death, which is the wages of sin, had no power over Him and no right to Him. Therefore, He could not stay dead, but He had to be resurrected. In justice, the Father could not allow His perfect Son to stay dead.

Jesus voluntarily laid down His life (John 10:18) and bore the penalty for our sins and died, but once the atonement was complete (John 19:30) and God's justice was satisfied, the sinless Lamb had to be raised from the dead. It was "impossible for death to keep its hold on Him?

A common question in the minds of many Christians is: If Jesus fully paid the price for our sins when He died, then why did He stay dead for several days and nights? Why didn't Jesus die and then immediately return to life? Why several days and nights in the tomb? There are many reasons why Jesus remained dead for several days and nights, and they are as follows:

- Jesus had to remain dead for a period of time that was long enough to show that He had truly died.

- The Word of God cannot be broken but must come to pass. Jesus had to fulfill the Old Testament Scriptures, as well as His own words, the He would be dead for several days and nights (1 Corinthians 15:4; Matthew 12:39-40; Luke 24:46; Hosea 6:2 our resurrection is in Christ and in His resurrection; Matthew 16:21; 17:23; John 2:19).

- Jesus remained dead for several days and nights because God, in His wisdom, simply decided that it would be that way.

Without Jesus' resurrection, there is no salvation.

> **1 Corinthians 15:17** (NKJV) [17] And if Christ is not risen, your faith *is* futile; you are still in your sins!

If Christ was not resurrected bodily, then our faith is in vain or fruitless, and we are still under the guilt of our sins and in a state of eternal condemnation.

If Jesus was not raised from the dead, He must have been sinful on the cross, and therefore, death had power over Him and a legal right to Him. This in turn means that He could not have died for anyone other than

Himself. Therefore, there was no vicarious death of an innocent substitute on our behalf, and we all must pay the eternal penalty for our sins ourselves.

Jesus, however, was sinless and holy on the cross; therefore, He was resurrected bodily (Luke 24:36-43). Consequently, we are not still in our sins; we have been saved, and we are born again unto a living hope of the complete manifestation of our redemption and of our future union with Jesus in His resurrection. Thus, Jesus' resurrection is the pledge and guarantee of our own resurrection....

> **John 14:19** (NKJV) [19] "A little while longer and the world will see Me no more, but you will see Me. Because I live, you will live also.

Jesus was the "firstborn from the dead."

> **Revelation 1:5** (NKJV) [5] and from Jesus Christ, the faithful witness, the firstborn from the dead, and the ruler over the kings of the earth. To Him who loved us and washed us from our sins in His own blood,

Jesus is called "firstborn" in Scripture in several different senses:

- Jesus was the "firstborn son" of His mother (Luke 2:7, 22-23). Jesus had brothers and sisters (Mathew 13:55-56), but He was the firstborn.

- The term "firstborn from among the dead" (Colossians 1:18) refers to Jesus' physical resurrection from the dead. He was the first man ever to be raised from the dead with a glorified body, never to die again (Acts 26:23).

  The fact that Jesus is "the firstborn from the dead" means more than that He was the first to be resurrected from the dead, never to die again. The expression also refers to the fact that His resurrection had secured the resurrection of His people, and is both the pledge and the pattern of it.

In another spiritual picture or figure, Christ is called "the firstfruits" of the dead in 1 Corinthians 15:20 and 23. The firstfruits in the Old Testament was that part of the harvest that was given to God to represent the dedication of the entire harvest to Him. The giving of the firstfruits to God was both an act of worship and of triumph, for the appearing of the firstfruits at the appointed time gave assurance that the rest of the harvest would be gathered safely in. In like manner, the resurrection of Jesus gives assurance as well as grounds for the resurrection of the full harvest of His redeemed into the kingdom.

- The term "firstborn" in Scripture refers not merely to birth but also to position, status and inheritance rights.

In Israel, the firstborn son had special rights and privileges including a larger share of the inheritance. In Exodus 4:22 and Jeremiah 31:9, the nation of Israel is called God's "firstborn," meaning that the nation was chosen by God to be the recipient of special privileges and blessings, as compared with the Gentile nations.

This usage of the term "firstborn" as meaning the most illustrious of its class is found in other places. In Job 18:13, "Deth's firstborn" is a deadly disease. In Isaiah 14:30, the "firstborn of the poor" (KJV) means a pauper of paupers. In Psalm 89:27, "I will also appoint him my firstborn," means to invest Him with royal dignity and clothe Him with preeminent splendor so as to make Him exalted in majesty above the kings of the earth.

This is the sense in which Christ is called the "firstborn" (Romans 8:29; Colossians 1:15; Hebrews 1:6). The term refers to His position, rank, rights and special privileges.

Colossians 1:15-16 (NKJV) [15] He is the image of the invisible God, the firstborn over all creation. [16] For by Him all things were created that are in heaven and that are on earth, visible and invisible, whether thrones or dominions or principalities or powers. All things were created through Him and for Him.

In Colossians 1:15-16, Paul's meaning is that because Jesus is the Creator of all things, He has the position of "firstborn" with respect to all creation. The term does not in any way refer to Jesus being "created" or "born" in any sense, but it speaks of His exalted position and precedence. Jesus holds the rank, as compared with every created thing, of firstborn in dignity and preeminence.

Paul moves from speaking of the preeminence of the Son in the whole universe in verse 15 to His preeminence as Head of the church in verse 18, and again uses the term "firstborn":

Colossians 1:18 (NKJV) [18] And He is the head of the body, the church, who is the beginning, the firstborn from the dead, that in all things He may have the preeminence.

So to refer to Jesus as the "firstborn from the dead" refers to the fact that He was the first man ever to be raised from the dead with a glorified body, never to die again. The term also refers to His exalted position and preeminence as the Son of God.

Jesus was "justified" by His resurrection.

1 Timothy 3:16 (NKJV) [16] And without controversy great is the mystery of godliness: God was manifested in the flesh, Justified in the Spirit, Seen by angels, Preached among the Gentiles, Believed on in the world, Received up in glory.

Paul, referring here to Jesus's resurrection, says Jesus was "justified in the spirit." Paul meant that by Jesus' resurrection from the dead it was shown or declared that He always was righteous in His spirit. By His resurrection, Jesus was declared to be the holy Son of God:

> **Romans 1:3-4** (NKJV) [3] concerning His Son Jesus Christ our Lord, who was born of the seed of David according to the flesh, [4] and declared *to be* the Son of God with power according to the Spirit of holiness, by the resurrection from the dead.

The Greek term for "justify" always means to declare to be righteous. For example, when a Christian is "justified," he is not "made" righteous in a literal sense. Righteousness is imputed to him or charged to his account, and he is declared by God to be righteous. Paul makes it clear in Romans 4 that righteousness is imputed to the Christian:

> **Romans 4:22-24** (NKJV) [22] And therefore *"it was accounted to him for righteousness."* [23] Now it was not written for his sake alone that it was imputed to him, [24] but also for us. It shall be imputed to us who believe in Him who raised up Jesus our Lord from the dead, [cf. v. 11]

The Christian's change of nature occurs in "regeneration" (John 1:12-13; Titus 3:5). Justification is a purely legal act of declaration in the "Courts of Heaven," whereas regeneration is a transforming act of the Holy Spirit on the inside of the believer.

Many Scriptures reveal the declarative nature of justification:

> **Genesis 44:16** (NKJV) [16] Then Judah said, "What shall we say to my lord? What shall we speak? Or how shall we clear ourselves? God has found out the iniquity of your servants; here we are, my lord's slaves, both we and *he* also with whom the cup was found."

> **Deuteronomy 25:1** (NKJV) [1] "If there is a dispute between men, and they come to court, that *the judges* may judge them, and they justify the righteous and condemn the wicked,

Job 9:20 (NKJV) [20] Though I were righteous, my own mouth would condemn me; Though I *were* blameless, it would prove me perverse.

Job 32:2 (NKJV) [2] Then the wrath of Elihu, the son of Barachel the Buzite, of the family of Ram, was aroused against Job; his wrath was aroused because he justified himself rather than God.

Matthew 11:19 (NKJV) [19] The Son of Man came eating and drinking, and they say, 'Look, a glutton and a winebibber, a friend of tax collectors and sinners!' But wisdom is justified by her children."

Luke 10:29 (NKJV) [29] But he, wanting to justify himself, said to Jesus, "And who is my neighbor?"

In all of the above Scriptures, the declarative meaning of the term "justification" is quite obvious. In this same sense, Jesus was "justified." By His resurrection from the dead, it was declared or proved that He always was righteous in His spirit (Rom. 1:3-4).

Some graves were opened at Jesus' death.

Matthew 27:50-53 (NKJV) [50] And Jesus cried out again with a loud voice, and yielded up His spirit. [51] Then, behold, the veil of the temple was torn in two from top to bottom; and the earth quaked, and the rocks were split, [52] and the graves were opened; and many bodies of the saints who had fallen asleep were raised; [53] and coming out of the graves after His resurrection, they went into the holy city and appeared to many.

In Matthew 27, the graves of the saints were opened when Jesus died, but their bodies came out of the graves only after Jesus' resurrection. It is likely that God intended this to signify that while it was Jesus' death that conquered our death and opened the door to physical immortality, it is in union with His resurrection that we are raised. Thus, while our redemption was wholly accomplished by the shed blood of Jesus, without His bodily resurrection we could not be saved.

Jonah's experience was a type of Jesus' death, burial and resurrection.

> **Matthew 12:38-40** (NKJV) [38] Then some of the scribes and Pharisees answered, saying, "Teacher, we want to see a sign from You." [39] But He answered and said to them, "An evil and adulterous generation seeks after a sign, and no sign will be given to it except the sign of the prophet Jonah. [40] For as Jonah was three days and three nights in the belly of the great fish, so will the Son of Man be three days and three nights in the heart of the earth.

The experience of the prophet Jonah was a type of Jesus' death, burial and resurrection. Jesus referred to His physical body being in the tomb for three days and nights as the fulfillment of that type.

In John 2:18-22, Jesus spoke of the same "sign" of His divine commission that He referred to in Matthew 12.

> **John 2:18-22** (NKJV) [18] So the Jews answered and said to Him, "What sign do You show to us, since You do these things?" [19] Jesus answered and said to them, "Destroy this temple, and in three days I will raise it up." [20] Then the Jews said, "It has taken forty-six years to build this temple, and will You raise it up in three days?" [21] But He was speaking of the temple of His body. [22] Therefore, when He had risen from the dead, His disciples remembered that He had said this to them; and they believed the Scripture and the word which Jesus had said.

The resurrection of Jesus' body after three days and nights in the grave was the sign of His divine commission. It was proof that God had sent Him to Israel.

We are called to be witnesses of Jesus' resurrection.

> **Acts 2:32** (NKJV) [32] This Jesus God has raised up, of which we are all witnesses.

Christians have been given a commission by God to be witnesses of the death and resurrection of Jesus Christ (Luke 24:46-48; Acts 1:21-22; 3:15; 4:33; 5:30-32; 13:27-31).

Jesus died on the cross to pay the penalty for our sins, but He did not stay dead. He rose from the dead, and He is alive today. Moreover, He is the same today as He was almost 2000 years ago:

> **Hebrews 13:8** (NKJV) [8] Jesus Christ *is* the same yesterday, today, and forever.

When Jesus was on the earth, He "went around doing good and healing all who were under the power of the devil" (Acts 10:38). Jesus is alive, and He is the same today; He is still saving and healing people and setting people free. He is still transforming lives. The only difference is that now He is doing it through His witness.

In Acts 1:8, Jesus commanded His disciples to be His witnesses:

> **Acts 1:8** (NKJV) [8] But you shall receive power when the Holy Spirit has come upon you; and you shall be witnesses to Me in Jerusalem, and in all Judea and Samaria, and to the end of the earth."

Many Christians today are trying to obey this command. However, a great many of them have ignored the fact that before Jesus commanded His disciples to be His witnesses, He told them to wait for the promise of the Father which was the baptism in the Holy Spirit after which they would "receive power." Again, in Luke 24:49, Jesus told His disciples to wait "until you have been clothed with power from on high."

Christians have been commissioned by God to be witnesses of the resurrection of Jesus, and the scriptural way to be a witness of Jesus is through the power of God:

> **Acts 4:33** (NKJV) [33] And with great power the apostles gave witness to the resurrection of the Lord Jesus. And great grace was upon them all.

We are to be witnesses of the resurrection of Jesus. We are not called to be witnesses just of the doctrine of His resurrection, but of His resurrection itself! Jesus is alive! Jesus is alive, and He is the same today as He always was. We are to be witnesses of the living Christ!

Therefore, we must have the same supernatural power of God in our lives to discharge our commission fully. Without the power of God, we shall be witnesses just to a church or to a creed or to another religion called "Christianity." However, with the power of the Holy Spirit, we shall be witnesses to a Person, to a living Person, the Lord Jesus Christ (Phil. 3:10).

Jesus did not command us to proclaim the "Gospel" to all nations without telling us what the "Gospel" is! A wonderful definition of the Gospel is found in Romans 1:16:

> **Romans 1:16** (NKJV) [16] For I am not ashamed of the gospel of Christ, for it is the power of God to salvation for everyone who believes, for the Jew first and also for the Greek.

The Gospel is the power of God for salvation, transformation of life, healing and deliverance to everyone who believes. The Gospel is the redemption of the whole man by the power of God through the death and resurrection of the Lord Jesus. Jesus is alive, and He has sent us to proclaim and to demonstrate His resurrection and His life.

The proofs of Jesus' resurrection are many:

- The experience of the guards at the tomb (Matthew 28:2-4, 11-15).

- The undisturbed grave clothing (John 20:2-10).

- The numerous appearances of Jesus after His resurrection. Jesus appeared to: Mary (John 20:16); the two disciples on the Road to Emmaeus (Luke 24); the other women (Matthew 28:9-10); Peter (Luke 24:34-35); the disciples with Thomas absent (Luke 24); the eleven disciples the following Sunday (John 20); the other 500 at one time in Galilee (1 Corinthians 15:6); James (1 Corinthians 15:7); and His last appearance at His ascension (Luke 24:51; Acts 1:9-12). Also included are: Paul (Acts 9); Stephen (Acts 7:55); and many people down through history, including numerous people today.

- The zealous fervor of the disciples who went all over the world preaching the resurrection. Today our lives should exhibit the same passion for our risen Lord!

- The change of the day of rest from the Sabbath (Saturday) to "The Lord's Day" (Sunday) in commemoration of Jesus' resurrection (Acts 20:7; 1 Corinthians 16:2; Revelation 1:10; cf. John 20:1).

- The Christian's own personal experience of faith assures him of Jesus' resurrection (1 John 5:10).

THE RESURRECTION OF MEN

Many men have been resurrected in the past. Both testaments record a number of resurrections (e.g., 2 Kings 13:21; John 11:44).

Furthermore, there have been many incidents in history of people who have been raised from the dead, including a large number in this century. However, in all those cases the people went on to die again. Their resurrection consisted of their physical body being restored to life. This is not the nature of the final resurrection. In the final resurrection, men and women will be resurrected bodily never to die again. Many Scriptures reveal that both the righteous and the lost will be resurrected bodily:

> **Daniel 12:2** (NKJV) [2] And many of those who sleep in the dust of the earth shall awake, Some to everlasting life, Some to shame *and* everlasting contempt.

> **John 5:28-30** (NKJV) [28] Do not marvel at this; for the hour is coming in which all who are in the graves will hear His voice [29] and come forth— those who have done good, to the resurrection of life, and those who have done evil, to the resurrection of condemnation. [30] I can of Myself do nothing. As I hear, I judge; and My judgment is righteous, because I do not seek My own will but the will of the Father who sent Me.

> **Acts 24:15** (NKJV) [15] I have hope in God, which they themselves also accept, that there will be a resurrection of *the* dead, both of *the* just and *the* unjust.

> **Revelation 20:5-6** (NKJV) [5] But the rest of the dead did not live again until the thousand years were finished. This *is* the first resurrection. [6] Blessed and holy *is* he who has part in the first resurrection. Over such the second death has no power, but they shall be priests of God and of Christ, and shall reign with Him a thousand years.

In addition to the above Scriptures, the bodily resurrection of the righteous is confirmed elsewhere in Scripture. For example:

> **John 6:39-40** (NKJV) [39] This is the will of the Father who sent Me, that of all He has given Me I should lose nothing, but should raise it up at the last day. [40] And this is the will of Him who sent Me, that everyone who sees the Son and believes in Him may have

everlasting life; and I will raise him up at the last day."

John 11:25-26 (NKJV) [25] Jesus said to her, "I am the resurrection and the life. He who believes in Me, though he may die, he shall live. [26] And whoever lives and believes in Me shall never die. Do you believe this?"

Romans 8:23 (NKJV) [23] Not only *that,* but we also who have the firstfruits of the Spirit, even we ourselves groan within ourselves, eagerly waiting for the adoption, the redemption of our body.

The bodily resurrection of the lost is taught also by the following passages:

Matthew 5:29-30 (NKJV) [29] If your right eye causes you to sin, pluck it out and cast *it* from you; for it is more profitable for you that one of your members perish, than for your whole body to be cast into hell. [30] And if your right hand causes you to sin, cut it off and cast *it* from you; for it is more profitable for you that one of your members perish, than for your whole body to be cast into hell.

Matthew 10:28 (NKJV) [28] And do not fear those who kill the body but cannot kill the soul. But rather fear Him who is able to destroy both soul and body in hell.

Jesus taught that the "body" of a man will be cast into eternal hell.

Revelation 20:13 (NKJV) [13] The sea gave up the dead who were in it, and Death and Hades delivered up the dead who were in them. And they were judged, each one according to his works.

The fact that the sea will give up the dead which are in it means their bodies will be resurrected.

THE NATURE OF THE RESURRECTION

The resurrection of the dead is not merely a "spiritual" resurrection in the sense of the spirit of a man living forever, but it will be a "bodily" resurrection.

Jesus' own resurrection was a bodily resurrection.

> **Luke 24:39** (NKJV) [39] Behold My hands and My feet, that it is I Myself. Handle Me and see, for a spirit does not have flesh and bones as you see I have."

And our future resurrection is said to be in the likeness of Jesus' resurrection.

> **Romans 6:5** (NKJV) [5] For if we have been united together in the likeness of His death, certainly we also shall be *in the likeness* of *His* resurrection,

> **Philippians 3:21** (NKJV) [21] who will transform our lowly body that it may be conformed to His glorious body, according to the working by which He is able even to subdue all things to Himself.

> **1 John 3:2** (NKJV) [2] Beloved, now we are children of God; and it has not yet been revealed what we shall be, but we know that when He is revealed, we shall be like Him, for we shall see Him as He is [cf. Romans 8:11; 2 Corinthians 4:14; Ephesians 1:19-20; Philippians 3:10-11].

When the righteous are resurrected, their bodies will be instantly and supernaturally changed into a new kind of body. This will happen at the time of Jesus' return to the earth:

> **1 Thessalonians 4:16-17** (NKJV) [16] For the Lord Himself will descend from heaven with a shout, with the voice of an archangel, and with the trumpet of God. And the dead in Christ will rise first. [17] Then we who are alive *and* remain shall be caught

up together with them in the clouds to meet the Lord in the air. And thus we shall always be with the Lord.

1 Corinthians 15:51-52 (NKJV) [51] Behold, I tell you a mystery: We shall not all sleep, but we shall all be changed— [52] in a moment, in the twinkling of an eye, at the last trumpet. For the trumpet will sound, and the dead will be raised incorruptible, and we shall be changed.

The lost will be resurrected at the time of the Great White Throne Judgment:

Revelation 20:4-5 (NKJV) [4] And I saw thrones, and they sat on them, and judgment was committed to them. Then *I saw* the souls of those who had been beheaded for their witness to Jesus and for the word of God, who had not worshiped the beast or his image, and had not received *his* mark on their foreheads or on their hands. And they lived and reigned with Christ for a thousand years. [5] But the rest of the dead did not live again until the thousand years were finished. This *is* the first resurrection.

Revelation 20:11-13 (NKJV) [11] Then I saw a great white throne and Him who sat on it, from whose face the earth and the heaven fled away. And there was found no place for them. [12] And I saw the dead, small and great, standing before God, and books were opened. And another book was opened, which is *the Book* of Life. And the dead were judged according to their works, by the things which were written in the books. [13] The sea gave up the dead who were in it, and Death and Hades delivered up the dead who were in them. And they were judged, each one according to his works.

THE GLORIFIED BODIES OF THE RESURRECTION

The fact that the righteous will be given new, glorified bodies is confirmed by Jesus in Matthew 22:

> **Matthew 22:29-32** (NKJV) [29] Jesus answered and said to them, "You are mistaken, not knowing the Scriptures nor the power of God. [30] For in the resurrection they neither marry nor are given in marriage, but are like angels of God in heaven. [31] But concerning the resurrection of the dead, have you not read what was spoken to you by God, saying, [32] *'I am the God of Abraham, the God of Isaac, and the God of Jacob'* ? God is not the God of the dead, but of the living."

The nature of our new bodies is described at length by Paul in 1 Corinthians 15:

> **1 Corinthians 15:35-38** (NKJV) [35] But someone will say, "How are the dead raised up? And with what body do they come?" [36] Foolish one, what you sow is not made alive unless it dies. [37] And what you sow, you do not sow that body that shall be, but mere grain—perhaps wheat or some other *grain.* [38] But God gives it a body as He pleases, and to each seed its own body.

From these verses, we see that while there is a direct continuity between the body that is buried and the body that is resurrected, the resurrected body will undergo definite and obvious changes.

> **1 Corinthians 15:39-40** (NKJV) [39] All flesh *is* not the same flesh, but *there is* one *kind of* flesh of men, another flesh of animals, another of fish, *and* another of birds. [40] There are also celestial bodies and terrestrial bodies; but the glory of the celestial *is* one, and the *glory* of the terrestrial *is* another.

Paul points out here that there is already a precedent in nature for the idea of different kinds of bodies. Out glorified bodies will be different from our natural, fleshly bodies.

1 Corinthians 15:41-42 (NKJV) [41] There is one glory of the sun, another glory of the moon, and another glory of the stars; for *one* star differs from *another* star in glory. [42] So also *is* the resurrection of the dead. *The body* is sown in corruption, it is raised in incorruption.

Paul states that there will be a difference between the glorified bodies of the redeemed. They will all be the same kind of glorified body, but there will be many different orders of glory among them. This same idea is found in Daniel 12:

Daniel 12:3 (NKJV) [3] Those who are wise shall shine Like the brightness of the firmament, And those who turn many to righteousness Like the stars forever and ever.

Then in 1 Corinthians 15, Paul goes on concerning the resurrection of our bodies:

1 Corinthians 15:42-53 (NKJV) [42] So also *is* the resurrection of the dead. *The body* is sown in corruption, it is raised in incorruption. [43] It is sown in dishonor, it is raised in glory. It is sown in weakness, it is raised in power. [44] It is sown a natural body, it is raised a spiritual body. There is a natural body, and there is a spiritual body. [45] And so it is written, *"The first man Adam became a living being."* The last Adam *became* a life-giving spirit. [46] However, the spiritual is not first, but the natural, and afterward the spiritual. [47] The first man *was* of the earth, *made* of dust; the second Man *is* the Lord from heaven. [48] As *was* the *man* of dust, so also *are* those *who are made* of dust; and as *is* the heavenly *Man,* so also *are* those *who are* heavenly. [49] And as we have borne the image of the *man* of dust, we shall also bear the image of the heavenly *Man.* [50] Now this I say, brethren, that flesh and blood cannot inherit the kingdom of God; nor does corruption inherit incorruption. [51] Behold, I tell you a mystery: We shall not all sleep, but we shall all be changed— [52] in a moment, in the twinkling of an eye, at the last trumpet. For the trumpet will sound, and the dead will be raised incorruptible, and we shall be changed. [53] For this corruptible must put on incorruption, and this mortal *must* put on immortality.

Paul speaks of five distinctive changes that will happen to the bodies of the righteous when they are resurrected:

1. The present body is perishable. It is subject to sickness, decay and old age. The new body will be imperishable and free from all these things.

2. The old body is a body of "dishonor." Its physical needs and limitations are, in a sense, a humiliation to man and a reminder of his fallen, sinful state. Paul calls our bodies "lowly" in Philippians 3:21. In contrast, the new body will have beauty and glory and be free from all of man's present limitations.

3. The present body dies in "weakness," but the new body will come forth from the grave by the supernatural power of God.

4. The old body is a "natural" body and is "of the dust of the earth" (1 Cor. 15:47), but the new body is a "spiritual body." This is not a "spirit body", but a body made of "spiritual material." In His glorified body, Jesus could walk through closed doors. He could travel at will. He could disappear if He wanted to. He could ascend to heaven and descend again to earth. He could eat if He wanted to for the enjoyment, but did not have to for the sake of His body. In all of these respects and in others not yet revealed, we will have the same kind of body that Jesus had!

5. The present body is "mortal" and subject to death. The new body will be "immortal" and incapable of death.

But what about the bodies of the lost? With what kind of body will they be resurrected?   We do not have the same extent of revelation concerning that, but we do have a little:

> **Daniel 12:2** (NKJV) [2] And many of those who sleep in the dust of the earth shall awake, Some to everlasting life, Some to shame *and* everlasting contempt.

> **Matthew 5:29-30** (NKJV) [29] If your right eye causes you to sin, pluck it out and cast *it* from you; for it is more profitable for you that one of your members perish, than for your whole body to be cast into hell. [30] And if your right hand causes you to sin, cut it off and cast *it* from you; for it is more profitable for you that one of your members perish, than for your whole body to be cast into hell.

Several things are clear from these verses.

1. The resurrected body of the lost will be one of "shame and contempt."

2. It will be a body capable of suffering the most agonizing pain and torment possible.

3. It will be an enduring body. The sufferings of hell will not consume it and bring it to an end, and the bodily sufferings of the lost will endure for eternity.

Chapter 12

ETERNAL JUDGMENT

We have now come to the last of the six foundational principles. In the Old Testament, the word "judgment" is used in two ways. It refers to the statutes, testimonies, and the law of God, and is usually in the plural. The other way it is used is in dealing with "God's judgments on the affairs of men and nations both in history and at the end of history".

There are two things that are certain to happen to every man and woman: death and judgment. No one can escape from either of these.

> **Hebrews 9:27** (NKJV) [27] And as it is appointed for men to die once, but after this the judgment,

> **Acts 17:30-31** (NKJV) [30] Truly, these times of ignorance God overlooked, but now commands all men everywhere to repent, [31] because He has appointed a day on which He will judge the world in righteousness by the Man whom He has ordained. He has given assurance of this to all by raising Him from the dead."

God will one day "judge the world with justice." That is why He commands all men to repent – because all men will be judged.

It is not just fallen man who will be judged, but all Christians will be judged too:

> **Romans 14:10** (NKJV) [10] But why do you judge your brother? Or why do you show contempt for your brother? For we shall all stand before the judgment seat of Christ.

All men and woman, saved and lost, will be resurrected, and after the resurrection, they will face judgment.

> **2 Corinthians 5:10** (NKJV) [10] For we must all appear before the judgment seat of Christ, that each one may receive the things *done* in the body, according to what he has done, whether good or bad.

Paul says that man's judgment will be of "the things done while in the body." This is why the resurrection of the body comes first. Man will be resurrected bodily and restored to his original state of wholeness – spirit, soul, mind and body – and then he will give an account for the actions he did while physically alive on the earth.

THE NATURE OF SIN

Sin can be against other men (Matthew 18:15; cf. v. 21; Genesis 42:22). Sin can be against yourself (Numbers 16:38; cf. Proverbs 6:32; 8:36; Jeremiah 44:7). However, all sin is ultimately against God:

> **Leviticus 6:2** (NKJV) [2] "If a person sins and commits a trespass against the LORD by lying to his neighbor about what was delivered to him for safekeeping, or about a pledge, or about a robbery, or if he has extorted from his neighbor, ... "

> **Psalm 51:4** (NKJV) [4] Against You, You only, have I sinned, And done *this* evil in Your sight— That You may be found just when You speak, *And* blameless when You judge.

> Cf. Genesis 20:6; 39:9; Leviticus 5:19; Numbers 5:6-7; 2 Samuel 12:9-10, 13; Ezra 10:2; Psalm 5:10; Jeremiah 14:20; 44:23; 51:5; Micah 7:9; Ephesians 1:17; Luke 15:21 "against heaven," i.e., against God

Sin is not just a passive weakness or simple imperfection in man. Sin is, in a sense, actively and violently opposed to God Himself. All sin is "against God," and this is why sin must be confessed to God. He is the One who will judge man for his sin, and He is the One who forgives sin:

> **Mark 2:7** (NKJV) [7] "Why does this *Man* speak blasphemies like this? Who can forgive sins but God alone?"

Sin is a violent contradiction to and "oppose" of God – of His own Being. All sin is a violation of God's own nature and being, and therefore, all sin must be punished by God.

"Punishment is the constitutional reaction of God's being against moral evil – the self-assertion of infinite holiness against its antagonist and would-be destroyer. In God this demand is devoid of all passion, and is consistent with infinite benevolence. It is a demand that cannot be evaded, since the holiness from which it springs is unchanging." (From Strong's *Systematic Theology*.)

> **Romans 1:18** (NKJV) [18] For the wrath of God is revealed from heaven against all ungodliness and unrighteousness of men, who suppress the truth in unrighteousness,

God's wrath and righteous anger will be poured out upon all sin and upon all sinners. All men, rich and poor, great and small, famous and unknown, have sinned against God and are under His wrath. No one can escape. This is why God commands all men everywhere to repent (Acts 17:30) and why all men must be born again (John 3:3, 7).

God will not compromise with sin; He cannot compromise with sin. Light does not ever compromise with darkness. It extinguishes it. God does not ever compromise with sin. He punishes it.

Sin will be punished. All men have sinned. Therefore, all men are, from conception, abiding under the punishment of sin – the eternal punishment of sin. But for God's gracious provision of forgiveness through the cross, this is the condition of all mankind: lost forever without hope.

THE MEANING OF JUDGMENT

The word "to judge" means "to separate; to make a distinction between; to exercise judgment upon; to estimate; to assume a censorial power over; to call to account; to bring under question; to judge judiciously; to try as a judge; to bring to trial; to sentence; to be brought to account; to administer government over; to govern."

GOD IS THE JUDGE OF ALL

The Scriptures present God as the moral Judge of the universe:

> **Genesis 18:25** (NKJV) [25] Far be it from You to do such a thing as this, to slay the righteous with the wicked, so that the righteous should be as the wicked; far be it from You! Shall not the Judge of all the earth do right?"

> **Psalm 50:6** (NKJV) [6] Let the heavens declare His righteousness, For God Himself *is* Judge. Selah

> **Hebrews 12:23** (NKJV) [23] to the general assembly and church of the firstborn *who are* registered in heaven, to God the Judge of all, to the spirits of just men made perfect,

> Cf. Psalm 9:8; 58:11; 94:2; Romans 2:5-6

Unrighteous judges may ignore sin, but God is a righteous Judge. God will not forget about sin and act as if it never happened. God will always punish sin, even the least sin. By the necessity of His own nature and being, God must punish sin.

God is perfectly just and righteous. As such, He must give to everyone his due with unvarying impartiality:

> **Matthew 16:27** (NKJV) [27] For the Son of Man will come in the glory of His Father with His angels, and then He will reward each according to his works.
>
> Cf. Nehemiah 9:33; Job 8:3, 20; 34:10-12; Proverbs 24:12; Jeremiah 17:10; 32:19; Romans 2:6

This does not mean that God enjoys punishing sinful man. Rather, the Scripture presents God as longsuffering, merciful and slow to judge.

Ezekiel 18:32 reveals the heart of God:

> **Ezekiel 18:32** (NKJV) [32] For I have no pleasure in the death of one who dies," says the Lord GOD. "Therefore turn and live!"
>
> **2 Peter 3:9** (NKJV) [9] The Lord is not slack concerning *His* promise, as some count slackness, but is longsuffering toward us, not willing that any should perish but that all should come to repentance.
>
> Cf. Psalm 86:5, 15; 100:5; Jeremiah 4:27-28; Lamentations 3:31-33; Ezekiel 18:23; 31:15; Matthew 18:14; Luke 6:35; 19:41-44; John 3:17; 1st Timothy 2:3-4; 2 Peter 3:9b; 1 John 4:8b)

God does not enjoy judging sinful men, but He will do it nevertheless.

THE PRINCIPLES OF DIVINE JUDGMENT

1. **God will judge all men.**

   1 Peter 1:17 (NKJV) [17] And if you call on the Father, who without partiality judges according to each one's work, conduct yourselves throughout the time of your stay *here* in fear;

Romans 2:5-6 (NKJV) [5] But in accordance with your hardness and your impenitent heart you are treasuring up for yourself wrath in the day of wrath and revelation of the righteous judgment of God, [6] who *"will render to each one according to his deeds"*:

No one will escape. Flattery or bribery will not work. Every man, woman and child who has ever lived will be judged.

2. God's judgment is according to truth.

Romans 2:2 (NKJV) [2] But we know that the judgment of God is according to truth against those who practice such things.

Man's judgment can be based upon a multitude of things, but God's judgment is consistent; it is always according to truth.

Jesus said that God's Word is truth (John 17:17), so God's judgment is according to His Word:

> **John 12:47-48** (NKJV) [47] And if anyone hears My words and does not believe, I do not judge him; for I did not come to judge the world but to save the world. [48] He who rejects Me, and does not receive My words, has that which judges him— the word that I have spoken will judge him in the last day.

All men will one day be judged by the impartial, unchanging standard of the Word of God.

3. God will judge every man's deeds.

Romans 2:6 (NKJV) [6] who *"will render to each one according to his deeds"*:

1 Peter 1:17 (NKJV) [17] And if you call on the Father, who without partiality judges according to each one's work, conduct yourselves throughout the time of your stay *here* in fear;

Matthew 12:36-37 (NKJV) ³⁶ But I say to you that for every idle word men may speak, they will give account of it in the day of judgment. ³⁷ For by your words you will be justified, and by your words you will be condemned."

Revelation 20:12 gives an account of the final judgment:

Revelation 20:12 (NKJV) ¹² And I saw the dead, small and great, standing before God, and books were opened. And another book was opened, which is *the Book* of Life. And the dead were judged according to their works, by the things which were written in the books.

The "books" described here are apparently the records of the deeds of all the lost. No act will be forgotten or hidden. Everything will be disclosed and judged.

Revelation 22:12 (NKJV) ¹² "And behold, I am coming quickly, and My reward *is* with Me, to give to every one according to his work.

4.   **God will judge the hidden motives of the heart.**

Ecclesiastes 12:14 (NKJV) ¹⁴ For God will bring every work into judgment, including every secret thing, whether good or evil.

Romans 2:16 (NKJV) ¹⁶ in the day when God will judge the secrets of men by Jesus Christ, according to my gospel.

1 Corinthians 4:5 (NKJV) ⁵ Therefore judge nothing before the time, until the Lord comes, who will both bring to light the hidden things of darkness and reveal the counsels of the hearts. Then each one's praise will come from God.

God will not only judge the outward actions of men; He will also judge every thought, intention and motive of their hearts.

Hebrews 4:13 (NKJV) ¹³ And there is no creature hidden from His sight, but all things *are* naked and open to the eyes of Him to whom we *must give* account.

5. **God will judge without partiality.**

   1 Peter 1:17 (NKJV) [17] And if you call on the Father, who without partiality judges according to each one's work, conduct yourselves throughout the time of your stay *here* in fear;

When men judge one another, they are often influenced by outward things such as race, physical appearance, education, wealth, social position, profession, etc. However, when God judges men, He will not be influenced by any of these things. His judgment will be perfect and impartial.

   Romans 2:11 (NKJV) [11] For there is no partiality with God.

Judgment will be dealt out strictly and exactly, justly and fairly by God.

6. **God will judge men according to the "light" that He made available to them.**

   Romans 2:12 (NKJV) [12] For as many as have sinned without law will also perish without law, and as many as have sinned in the law will be judged by the law

This "light" includes both general moral understanding of right and wrong as well as the specific revelation of the Gospel. The greater the "light" one rejected, the greater his judgment. This principle is stated in Luke 12:

> Luke 12:47-48 (NKJV) [47] And that servant who knew his master's will, and did not prepare *himself* or do according to his will, shall be beaten with many *stripes.* [48] But he who did not know, yet committed things deserving of stripes, shall be beaten with few. For everyone to whom much is given, from him much will be required; and to whom much has been committed, of him they will ask the more.

Consider also the words of Jesus in Matthew 11:

> **Matthew 11:20-24** (NKJV) [20] Then He began to rebuke the cities in which most of His mighty works had been done, because they did not repent: [21] "Woe to you, Chorazin! Woe to you, Bethsaida! For if the mighty works which were done in you had been done in Tyre and Sidon, they would have repented long ago in sackcloth and ashes. [22] But I say to you, it will be more tolerable for Tyre and Sidon in the day of judgment than for you. [23] And you, Capernaum, who are exalted to heaven, will be brought down to Hades; for if the mighty works which were done in you had been done in Sodom, it would have remained until this day. [24] But I say to you that it shall be more tolerable for the land of Sodom in the day of judgment than for you."
>
> Cf. Luke 11:31-32

Jesus said that the wicked ancient cities of Tyre, Sidon and Sodom would receive a less severe judgment in the Last Day than the cities which heard and rejected His own preaching of the Gospel with signs and wonders.

So, we see that a man is not judged only by his works; he is also judged according to the knowledge of God and truth that he rejected. This has great significance when we consider the sin of the apostate who has known the truth of the Gospel and yet willfully turns from it after obeying it for a time. He turns away from God with his eyes wide open. Awful judgment awaits him. Peter says:

> **2 Peter 2:20-21** (NKJV) [20] For if, after they have escaped the pollutions of the world through the knowledge of the Lord and Savior Jesus Christ, they are again entangled in them and overcome, the latter end is worse for them than the beginning. [21] For it would have been better for them not to have known the way of righteousness, than having known *it,* to turn from the holy commandment delivered to them.

THE FINAL JUDGMENT AND ETERNAL PUNISHMENT

The Fact of Final Judgment

Scriptural Evidence for a Final Judgment. Scripture frequently affirms the fact that there will be a great final judgment of believers and unbelievers. They stand before the judgment seat of Christ in resurrected bodies and hear His proclamation of their eternal destiny.

The final judgment is vividly portrayed in John's vision in Revelation:

> **Revelation 20:11-15** (NKJV) [11] Then I saw a great white throne and Him who sat on it, from whose face the earth and the heaven fled away. And there was found no place for them. [12] And I saw the dead, small and great, standing before God, and books were opened. And another book was opened, which is *the Book* of Life. And the dead were judged according to their works, by the things which were written in the books. [13] The sea gave up the dead who were in it, and Death and Hades delivered up the dead who were in them. And they were judged, each one according to his works. [14] Then Death and Hades were cast into the lake of fire. This is the second death. [15] And anyone not found written in the Book of Life was cast into the lake of fire.

Many other passages teach this final judgment. Paul tells the Greek philosophers in Athens that God "Now . . . commands all men everywhere to repent, because *He has fixed a day on which He will judge the world in righteousness* by a man whom He has appointed, and of this He has given assurance to all men by raising Him from the dead" (Acts 17:30-31). Similarly, Paul talks about "the day of wrath when God's righteous judgment will be revealed" (Rom. 2:5). Other passages speak clearly of a coming day of judgment (see Matt. 10:15; 11:22, 24; 12:36; 25:31-46; 1 Cor. 4:5; Heb. 6:2; 2 Peter 2:4; Jude 6, et al.).

This final judgment is the culmination of many precursors in which God rewarded righteousness or punished unrighteousness throughout history. While He brought blessing and deliverance from danger to those who were faithful to Him, including Abel, Noah, Abraham, Isaac, Jacob, Moses, David, and the faithful among the people of Israel, He also from time to time brought judgment on those who persisted in disobedience and unbelief; His judgments included the flood, the dispersion of the people from the tower of Babel, the judgments on Sodom and Gomorrah, and continuing judgments throughout history, both on individuals (Rom. 1:18-32) and on nations (Isa. 13-23, et al.) who persisted in sin. Moreover, in the unseen spiritual realm He brought judgment on angels who sinned (2 Peter 2:4). Peter reminds us that God's judgments have been carried out periodically and with certainty, and this reminds us that a final judgment is yet coming, for "the Lord knows how to rescue the godly from trial, and to keep the unrighteousness under punishment until the day of judgment, and especially those who indulge in the lust of defiling passion and despise authority" (2 Peter 2:9-10).

Will There Be More Than One Judgment? According to a dispensational view, there is more than one judgment to come. For example, dispensationalists would not see the final judgment in Matthew 25:31-46:

> **Matthew 25:31-46** (NKJV) [31] "When the Son of Man comes in His glory, and all the holy angels with Him, then He will sit on the throne of His glory. [32] All the nations will be gathered before Him,
>
> and He will separate them one from another, as a shepherd divides *his* sheep from the goats. [33] And He will set the sheep on His right hand, but the goats on the left. [34] Then the King will say

to those on His right hand, 'Come, you blessed of My Father, inherit the kingdom prepared for you from the foundation of the world: [35] for I was hungry and you gave Me food; I was thirsty and you gave Me drink; I was a stranger and you took Me in; [36] I *was* naked and you clothed Me; I was sick and you visited Me; I was in prison and you came to Me.' [37] "Then the righteous will answer Him, saying, 'Lord, when did we see You hungry and feed *You,* or thirsty and give *You* drink? [38] When did we see You a stranger and take *You* in, or naked and clothe *You?* [39] Or when did we see You sick, or in prison, and come to You?' [40] And the King will answer and say to them, 'Assuredly, I say to you, inasmuch as you did *it* to one of the least of these My brethren, you did *it* to Me.' [41] "Then He will also say to those on the left hand, 'Depart from Me, you cursed, into the everlasting fire prepared for the devil and his angels: [42] for I was hungry and you gave Me no food; I was thirsty and you gave Me no drink; [43] I was a stranger and you did not take Me in, naked and you did not clothe Me, sick and in prison and you did not visit Me.' [44] "Then they also will answer Him, saying, 'Lord, when did we see You hungry or thirsty or a stranger or naked or sick or in prison, and did not minister to You?' [45] Then He will answer them, saying, 'Assuredly, I say to you, inasmuch as you did not do *it* to one of the least of these, you did not do *it* to Me.' [46] And these will go away into everlasting punishment, but the righteous into eternal life."

From a dispensational perspective, this passage does not refer to final judgment (the "great white throne judgment" spoken of in Rev. 20:11-15), but rather to a judgment that comes after the tribulation and before the beginning of the millennium. They say that this will be a "judgment of the nations" in which the nations

are judged according to how they have treated the Jewish people during the tribulation. Those who have treated the Jews well and are willing to submit to Christ will enter into the millennium, and those who have not will be refused entrance.

Thus, in a dispensational view there are different judgments: (a) a "judgment of the nations" (Mathew 25:31-46) to determine who enters the millennium; (b) a "judgment of believers' works" (sometimes called the *bema* judgment after the Greek word for "judgment seat" in 2 Cor. 5:10) in which Christians will receive degrees of reward; and (c) a "great white throne judgment" at the end of the millennium (Rev. 20:11-15) to declare eternal punishments for unbelievers.

The view taken in this book is that these three passages all speak of the same final judgment, not of three separate judgments. With regard to Matthew 25:31-46 in particular, it is unlikely that the dispensational view is correct: There is no mention of entering into the millennium in this passage. Moreover, the judgments pronounced speak not of entrance into the millennial kingdom on earth or exclusion from that kingdom but of eternal destinies of people: "Inherit that kingdom prepared for you from the foundation of the world . . . Depart from Me, you cursed, into the eternal fire prepared for the devil and his angels . . . And they will go away into *eternal punishment*, but the righteous into *eternal life*" (vv. 34, 41, 46). Finally, it would be inconsistent with God's ways throughout Scripture to deal with people's *eternal* destiny on the basis of what nation they belong to, for unbelieving nations have believers within them, and nations that exhibit more conformity to God's revealed will still have many wicked within them. And "God shows no partiality" (Rom. 2:11). Though indeed "all the nations" are gathered before Christ's throne in this scene (Matt. 25:32), the picture of judgment is one of judgment on individuals (sheep are separated from goats, and those individuals

who treated Christ's brothers kindly are welcomed into the kingdom while those who rejected them are rejected, vv. 35-40, 42-45).

The Time of Final Judgment

The final judgment will occur after the millennium and the rebellion that occurs at the end of it. John pictures the millennial kingdom and the removal of Satan from influence on the earth in Revelation 20:1-6. After God decisively defeats this final rebellion (Rev. 20:7-10), John tells us that judgment will follow: "Then I saw a great white throne and him who sat upon it" (v. 11).

The Nature of the Final Judgment

Jesus Christ Will Be the Judge. Paul Speaks of "Jesus Christ who is to judge the living and the dead" (2 Tim. 4:1). Peter says that Jesus Christ "is the one ordained by God to be the judge of the living and the dead" (Acts 10:42; compare 17:31; Matt. 25:31-33). This right to act as judge over the whole universe is something that the Father has given to the Son: "The Father . . . has given Him authority to execute judgment, because He is the Son of Man" (John 5:26-27).

Unbelievers Will Be Judged. It is clear that all unbelievers will stand before Christ for judgment, for this judgment includes "the dead, great and small" (Rev. 20:12), and Paul says that "on the day of wrath when God's righteous judgment will be revealed," "He will render to every man according to his works . . . for those who are factious and do not obey the truth, but obey wickedness, there will be wrath and fury" (Rom. 2:5-7).

This judgment of unbelievers will include *degrees of punishment*, for we read that the dead were judged "by what they had done" (Rev. 20:12, 13), and this judgment according to what people had done must therefore involve an evaluation of the works that people have done. Similarly, Jesus says:

> **Luke 12:47-48** (NKJV) [47] And that servant who knew his master's

will, and did not prepare *himself* or do according to his will, shall be beaten with many *stripes.* [48] But he who did not know, yet committed things deserving of stripes, shall be beaten with few. For everyone to whom much is given, from him much will be required; and to whom much has been committed, of him they will ask the more.

When Jesus says to the cities of Chorazin and Bethsaida, "It shall be *more tolerable* on the day of judgment for Tyre and Sidon than for you" (Matt. 11:22; compare v. 24), or when He says that the scribes "will receive the *greater condemnation*" (Luke 20:47), He implies that there will be degrees of punishment on the last day.

In fact, every wrong deed done will be remembered and taken account of in the punishment that is meted out on that day, because "on the day of judgment men will render account for every careless word they utter" (Matt. 12:36). Every word spoken, every deed done will be brought to light and receive judgment: "For God will bring every deed into judgment, with every secret thing, whether good or evil" (Eccl. 12:14).

As these verses indicate, on the day of judgment the secrets of people's hearts will be revealed and made public. Paul speaks of the day when "God judges the secrets of men by Christ Jesus" (Rom. 2:16; compare Luke 8:17). "Nothing is covered up that will not be revealed, or hidden that will not be known. Therefore *whatever you have said in the dark shall be heard in the light, and what you have whispered in private rooms shall be proclaimed upon the housetops*" (Luke 12:2-3).

Believers Will Be Judged. In writing to Christians Paul says, "*We shall all stand before the judgment seat of God* . . . Each of us shall give account of himself to God" (Rom. 14:10, 12). He also tells the Corinthians, "For *we must all appear before the judgment seat of Christ, that each one may receive what is due him for the things*

215

done while in the body, whether good or bad" (2 Cor. 5:10; cf. Rom. 2:6-11; Rev. 20:12, 15). In addition, the picture of the final judgment in Matthew 25:31-46 includes Christ separating the sheep from the goats, and rewarding those who receive His blessing.

It is important to realize that this judgment of believers will be a judgment to evaluate and bestow various degrees of reward, but the fact that they will face such a judgment should never cause believers to fear that they will be eternally condemned. Jesus says, "He who hears My word and believes Him who sent Me, has eternal life; *he does not come into judgment, but has passed from death to life*" (John 5:24). Here "judgment" must be understood in the sense of eternal condemnation and death, since it is contrasted with passing from death into life. At the day of final judgment more than at any other time, it is of utmost importance that "there is therefore now *no condemnation for those who are in Christ Jesus*" (Rom. 8:1). Thus the Day of Judgment can be portrayed as one in which believers are rewarded and unbelievers are punished:

> **Revelation 11:18** (NKJV) [18] The nations were angry, and Your wrath has come, And the time of the dead, that they should be judged, And that You should reward Your servants the prophets and the saints, And those who fear Your name, small and great, And should destroy those who destroy the earth."

Will all the secret words and deeds of believers, and all their sins, also be revealed on that last day? We might at first think so, because Paul says that when the Lord comes He will "*bring to light the things now hidden in darkness* and will disclose the purposes of the heart. Then every man will receive his commendation from God" (1 Cor. 4:5; compare Col. 3:25). However, this is a context that talks about "commendation," or praise (*epainos*), that comes from God, so it may not refer to sins. And other verses suggest that God will never again call our sins to remembrance:

"You will cast all our sins into the depths of the sea" (Mic. 7:19); "as far as the east is from the west, so far does He remove our transgressions from us" (Ps. 103:12); "*I will not remember your sins*" (Isa. 43:25); "*I will remember their sins no more*" (Heb. 8:12; compare 10:17).

Scripture also teaches that there will be *degrees of reward for believers*. Paul encourages the Corinthians to be careful how they build the church on the foundation that has already been laid – Jesus Christ Himself.

> **1 Corinthians 3:12-15** (NKJV) [12] Now if anyone builds on this foundation *with* gold, silver, precious stones, wood, hay, straw, [13] each one's work will become clear; for the Day will declare it, because it will be revealed by fire; and the fire will test each one's work, of what sort it is. [14] If anyone's work which he has built on *it* endures, he will receive a reward. [15] If anyone's work is burned, he will suffer loss; but he himself will be saved, yet so as through fire.

Paul similarly says of Christians that "we must all appear before the judgment seat of Christ, that each one may receive *what is due him for the things done while in the body*, whether good or bad" (2 Cor. 5:10), again implying degrees of reward for what we have done in this life. Likewise, in the parable of the minas, the one who made ten minas more was told, "You shall have authority over ten cities," and the one whose minas had made five minas more was told, "And you are to be over five cities" (Luke 19:17, 19). Many other passages likewise teach or imply degrees of reward for believers at the final judgment (Dan. 12:2; Matt. 6:10, 20-21, 19:21; Luke 6:22-23, 12:18-21, 32, 42-48; 14:13-14; 1 Cor. 3:8; 9:18; 13:3; 15:19, 29-32, 58; Gal. g:9-10; Eph. 6:7-8; Phil. 4:17; Col. 3:23-24; 1 Tim 6:18; Heb. 10:34, 35; 11:10, 14 16, 26, 35; 1 Peter 1.4; 2 John 8; Rev. 11:28; 22:12; cf. also Matt. 5:46; 6:2-6, 16-18, 24; Luke 6:35.)

But we must guard against misunderstanding here: Even though there will be degrees of reward in heaven, the joy of each person will be full and complete for eternity. If we ask how this can be when there are different degrees of reward, it simply shows that our perception of happiness is based on the assumption that happiness depends on what we possess or the status or power that we have.

In actuality, however, our true happiness consists of delighting in God and rejoicing in the status and recognition that He has given us. The foolishness of thinking that only those who have been highly rewarded and given great status will be fully happy in heaven is seen when we realize that no matter how great a reward we are given, there will always be those with greater rewards, or who have higher status and authority, including the apostles, the heavenly creatures, and Jesus Christ and God Himself.

Therefore if highest status was essential for people to be fully happy, no one but God would be fully happy in heaven, which is certainly an incorrect idea. Moreover, those with greater reward and honor in heaven, those nearest the throne of God, delight not in their status but only in the privilege of falling down before God's throne to worship Him (see Rev. 4:10-11).

It would be morally and spiritually beneficial for us to have a greater consciousness of this clear New Testament teaching on degrees of heavenly reward. Rather than making us competitive with one another, it would cause us to help and encourage one another that we all may increase our heavenly reward, for God has an infinite capacity to bring blessing to us all, and we are all members of one another (cf. 1 Cor. 12:26-27). We would more eagerly heed the admonition of the author of Hebrews, "*Let us consider how to stir up one another to love and good works*, not neglecting to meet together, as is the habit of some, but *encouraging one another*, and all the more as you see the Day drawing near" (Heb. 10:24-25).

Moreover, in our own lives a heartfelt seeking of future heavenly reward would motivate us to work wholeheartedly for the Lord at whatever task He calls us to, whether great or small, paid or unpaid. It would also make us long for His approval rather than for wealth or success. It would motivate us to work at building up the church on the one foundation Jesus Christ (1 Cor. 3:10-15).

Angels Will Be Judged. Peter says that the rebellious angels have been committed to pits of nether gloom "to be kept until the judgment" (2 Peter 2:4), and Jude says that rebellious angels have been kept by God "until the judgment of the great day" (Jude 6). This means that at least the *rebellious* angels or demons will be subject to judgment on the last day as well.

Scripture does not clearly indicate whether righteous angels will undergo some kind of evaluation of their service as well, but it is possible that they are included in Paul's statement "Do you not know that *we are to judge angels*?" (1 Cor. 6:3). It is probable that this includes righteous angels because there is no indication in the context that Paul is speaking of demons or fallen angels, and the word "angel" without further qualification in the New Testament would normally be understood to refer to righteous angels. But the text is not explicit enough to give us certainty.

We Will Help in the Work of Judgment. It is a rather amazing aspect of New Testament teaching that we (believers) will take part in the process of judgment. Paul says:

> **1 Corinthians 6:2-3** (NKJV) [2] Do you not know that the saints will judge the world? And if the world will be judged by you, are you unworthy to judge the smallest matters? [3] Do you not know that we shall judge angels? How much more, things that pertain to this life?

It might be argued that this simply means we will be watching the declaration of judgment by Christ and approving it, but this does not seem to fit the context well, for here Paul is encouraging the Corinthians to settle legal disputes among themselves rather than taking them to court before unbelievers. In this very context he says, "Can it be that there is no man among you wise enough to decide between members of the brotherhood, but brother goes to law against brother, and that before unbelievers?" (1 Cor. 6:5-6). This kind of judgment certainly involves careful evaluation and wise discernment. And this implies that such careful evaluation and discernment will be exercised by us in judging angels and in judging the world on the day of final judgment.

This is similar to the teaching of Revelation 20, where John says that he saw thrones, and "seated on them were *those to whom judgment was committed*" (Rev. 20:4). Although the text does not explain the identity of those seated on the thrones, the fact that they are mentioned in the plural indicates that Christ does not reserve every aspect of the process of judging for himself alone. Indeed, he tells his twelve disciples that they will "sit on twelve thrones, *judging* the twelve tribes of Israel" (Matt. 19:28; compare Luke 22:30). This accords with the fact that throughout the history of redemption God has from time to time given the right to exercise judgment into the hands of human authorities, whether Moses and the elders who assisted him, the judges of Israel whom God raised up during the period of the judges, the wise kings such as David and Solomon, the civil government of many nations (see Rom. 13:1-7; 1 Peter 2:13-14), or those who have authority to rule and govern within the church and to oversee the exercise of church discipline.

NECESSITY OF FINAL JUDGMENT

Since when believers die they pass immediately into the presence of God, and when unbelievers die they pass into a state of separation from God and the endurance of punishment, we may wonder why God has a time of final judgment established at all. Berkhof wisely points out that the final judgment is not for the purpose of letting God find out the condition of our hearts or the pattern of conduct of our lives, for He already knows that in every detail. Berkhof rather says of the final judgment:

It will serve the purpose rather of displaying before all rational creatures the declarative glory of God in a formal, forensic act, which magnifies on the one hand His holiness and righteousness, and on the other hand, His grace and mercy. Moreover, it should be borne in mind that the judgment at the last day will differ from that of the death of each individual in more than one respect. It will not be secret, but public; it will not pertain to the soul only, but also to the body; it will not have reference to a single individual, but to all men.

Justice of God in the Final Judgment

Scripture clearly affirms that God will be entirely just in his judgment and no one will be able to complain against him on that day. God is the one who "judges each one impartially according to his deeds" (1 Peter 1:17), and "God shows no partiality" (Rom. 2:11; compare Col. 3:25). For this reason, on the last day "every mouth will be stopped," and the whole world will be "held accountable to God" (Rom. 3:19), with no one being able to complain that God has treated him or her unfairly. In fact, one of the great blessings of the final judgment will be that saints and angels will see demonstrated in millions of lives the absolutely pure justice of God, and this will be a source of praise to Him for all eternity. At the time of the judgment on wicked Babylon, there will be great praise in heaven, crying, '*Hallelujah*! Salvation and glory and power belong to our God, *for His judgments are true and just*'" (Rev. 19:1-2).

FORMAL APPLICATION OF THE FINAL JUDGMENT

The doctrine of final judgment has several positive moral influences in our lives.

The Doctrine of Final Judgment Satisfies Our Inward Sense of a Need for Justice in the World. The fact that there will be a final judgment assures us that ultimately God's universe is *fair*, for God is in control, and He keeps accurate records and renders just judgment. When Paul tells slaves to be submissive to their masters, he assures them, "For the wrongdoer will be paid back for the wrong he has done, and there is no partiality" (Col. 3:25). When a picture of a final judgment mentions the fact that "books were opened" (Rev. 20:12; compare Mal. 3:16), it reminds us (whether the books are literal or symbolic) that a permanent and accurate record of all our deeds has been kept by God, and ultimately all accounts will be settled and all will be made right.

The Doctrine of Final Judgment Enables Us to Forgive Others Freely. We realize that it is not up to us to take revenge on others who have wronged us, or even to want to do so, because God has reserved that right for Himself. "Beloved, never avenge yourselves, but leave it to the wrath of God, for it is written, *'Vengeance is mine, I will repay, says the Lord'*" (Rom. 12:19). In this way whenever we have been wronged, we can give into God's hands any desire to harm or pay back the person who has wronged us, knowing that every wrong in the universe will ultimately be paid for – either it will turn out to have been paid for by Christ when He died on the cross (if the wrongdoer becomes a Christian), or it will be paid for at the final judgment (for those who do not trust in Christ for salvation). But in either case we can give the situation into God's hands, and then pray that the wrongdoer will trust Christ for salvation and thereby receive forgiveness of his or her sins. This thought should keep us from harboring bitterness or resentment in our hearts for injustices we have suffered that have not been made right: God is just, and we can leave these situations in His hands, knowing that He will someday right all wrongs and give absolutely fair rewards and punishments. In this way we are following in the example of Christ, who "when He was reviled, He did not revile in return; when He suffered, He did not threaten; but *He trusted to Him who judges justly*" (1 Peter 2:22-23). He also prayed, "Father, forgive them, for they know not what they do" (Luke 23:34; compare Acts 7:60, where Stephen followed Jesus' example in praying for those who put him to death).

The Doctrine of the Final Judgment Provides a Motive for Righteous Living. For believers, the final judgment is an incentive to faithfulness and good works, not as a means of earning forgiveness of sins, but as a means of gaining greater eternal reward. This is a healthy and good motive for us – Jesus tells us, "Lay up for yourselves treasures in heaven" (Matt. 6:20) – though it runs counter to the popular views of our secular culture, a culture that does not really believe in heaven or eternal rewards at all.

For unbelievers, the doctrine of final judgment still provides some moral restraint on their lives. If in a society there is a widespread general acknowledgment that all will someday give account to the Creator of the universe for their lives, some "fear of God" will characterize many people's lives. By contrast, those who have no deep consciousness of final judgment give themselves up to greater and greater evil, demonstrating that "there is *no fear of God* before their eyes" (Rom. 3:18). Those who deny the final judgment, Peter says, will be "scoffers" who "will come in the last days with scoffing, *following their own passions* and saying, 'Where is the promise of His coming?'" (2 Peter 3:3-4). He also declares that evildoers who "are surprised that you do not now join them in the same wild profligacy," and "who abuse you" will nonetheless "give account to Him who is ready to judge the living and the dead" (1 Peter 4:4-5). An awareness of final judgment is both a comfort to believers and a warning to unbelievers not to continue in their evil ways.

The Doctrine of Final Judgment Provides a Great Motive for Evangelism. The decisions made by people in this life will affect their destiny for all eternity, and it is right that our hearts feel and our mouths echo the

sentiment of the appeal of God through Ezekiel, "Turn back, turn back from your evil ways; for why will you die, O house of Israel?" (Ezek. 33:11). In fact, Peter indicates that the delay of the Lord's return is due to the fact that God "is forbearing toward you, not wishing that any should perish, but that all should reach repentance" (2 Peter 3:9).

THE NATURE OF THE ETERNAL PUNISHMENT OF THE LOST

The eternal sufferings of the lost consist of:

1.   Exclusion from the presence, favor and fellowship of God.

> *They will receive the punishment of eternal destruction as exiles from the presence of the Lord . . . (2 Thessalonians 1:9, Williams New Testament)*

God is infinite Spirit and is everywhere all at once. Therefore, "exclusion from the presence of God" does not mean there could ever exist a place where God is not (Jeremiah 23:24; Psalm 139:7-8). Nevertheless, it will be Jesus who says to the lost, "Depart from Me" (Matthew 7:23, KJV; cf. Psalm 5:4-6; Matthew 25:41; Luke 13:27; John 8:21; Revelation 21:27; 22:15), and so this signifies eternal alienation from God and total separation from His manifest presence and blessing.

This is the essence of the Fall, and it is the worst punishment that could ever come to man – the eternal and irrevocable loss of fellowship with his God. Man was made for God – for fellowship with Him. There will be no greater pain or anguish that comes to ruined mankind than that which results from this loss.

2.   The loss of all earthly good, enjoyment and pleasure.

> *...the mirth of the wicked is brief, the joy of the godless lasts but a moment. (Job 20:5; cf. Job 20:18; 27:8; Psalm 39:6; 49:10, 16-17; Ecclesiastes 2:18; 5:15; Luke 12:20; 16:25; Jeremiah 17:11)*

While upon the earth sinful man enjoys much that is good, but it is all only for a moment, a very brief space of time. An instant after death, all the good things he enjoyed in this life, all the social prestige and position he obtained, and all the material wealth he heaped to himself will be gone forever. In eternity, he will discover that the only abiding "wealth" he ever possessed and the only lasting "treasure" he ever laid hold of is the eternal wrath of God (Romans 2:5).

Another aspect of eternal suffering will be the inward despair and agony of those who are lost, forever, without hope. The despair and pain of being utterly and eternally without hope and fully knowing it is unimaginable. Arthur Pink wrote, "unrelieved will be the fearful sufferings; interminable their torments. No means of escape. No possibility of a reprieve. No hope of deliverance...'There is no peace, saith my God, to the wicked.' There will be no resting-place in hell; no secret corner where they can find a little respite; no cooling fountain at which they may refresh themselves. There will be no change or variation of their lot. Day and night, forever and ever, shall they be punished. With no prospect of any improvement they will sink down into blank despair."

3. **The fire.**

They will throw them into the fiery furnace, where there will be weeping and gnashing of teeth. (Matthew 13:42; cf. Matthew 5:22; 13:47-50; 18:8-9; 25:41; Luke 3:17)

The fire is obviously not a physical fire because Satan and his angels, who will suffer there as well, are spirit beings. It is, however, an actual fire except it is a spiritual one; it is a fire of spiritual substance. This spiritual fire will be far worse in its ability to inflict pain and suffering than a natural physical fire. It will be an eternal, undying fire.

> **Revelation 14:10-11** (NKJV) [10] he himself shall also drink of the wine of the wrath of God, which is poured out full strength into the cup of His indignation. He shall be tormented with fire and brimstone in the presence of the holy angels and in the presence

of the Lamb. [11] And the smoke of their torment ascends forever and ever; and they have no rest day or night, who worship the beast and his image, and whoever receives the mark of his name."

Cf. Mark 9:43; Jude 7; Revelation 20:10; 21:8

Mark 9:47-49 (NKJV) [47] And if your eye causes you to sin, pluck it out. It is better for you to enter the kingdom of God with one eye, rather than having two eyes, to be cast into hell fire— [48] where *'Their worm does not die And the fire is not quenched.'* [49] "For everyone will be seasoned with fire, and every sacrifice will be seasoned with salt.

In Mark 9:49, the phrase "everyone will be salted with fire" probably means that the unquenchable fire of the second death, instead of destroying as fire usually does, will act like salt and preserve in a state of torment and agony. Exodus 3:2 and Deuteronomy 5:23 give examples of how God can make a fire that will burn something and yet not destroy it, but preserve it in a state of burning.

The abode of the lost at present, which is in one region of hades, is a place of torment by fire as well (Luke 16:22-28). The testimonies of a number of people who have had supernatural visions and experiences of both hades and the eternal lake of fire confirm all of the above.

4. **The lake of fire is a place of extreme anguish and torment.**

Romans 2:8-9 (NKJV) [8] but to those who are self-seeking and do not obey the truth, but obey unrighteousness—indignation and wrath, [9] tribulation and anguish, on every soul of man who does evil, of the Jew first and also of the Greek;

Paul says the eternal state of the lost will consist in "trouble" and "distress." The Greek words translated "trouble" and "distress" respectively refer to outward affliction and inner torment. The suffering will be entire: spiritually, mentally, emotionally and bodily – every faculty of man will experience the severest, acutest agony possible to his heightened senses.

The lake of fire will be a place of the most awful suffering. Jesus referred to the "weeping and gnashing of teeth" of the lost no less than seven times in the Gospels (Matthew 8:12; 13:41-42, 49-50; 22:13; 24:51; 25:30; Luke 13:28). Weeping and gnashing of teeth are extreme expressions of sorrow and anguish.

Those in the lake of fire will be "tormented . . . forever and ever" (Revelation 14:10-11). The Greek word translated "tormented" in Revelation 14:10 means to "torture" or "torment"; it occurs for the first time in the New Testament in Matthew 8:6: "my servant lies at home paralyzed and in terrible suffering." The same word occurs again in Revelation 9:5 where it is said that during the Tribulation, the demonic "locusts" will be given the power to torment with "the sting of a scorpion when it strikes a man." This will cause a suffering so intense that men will "seek death, but will not find it; they will long to die, but death will elude them" (Revelation 9:6).

The pains and torments of hell will be far beyond the most excruciating pain that one is now capable of conceiving.

5. **The companions.**

   Matthew 25:41 (NKJV) [41] "Then He will also say to those on the left hand, 'Depart from Me, you cursed, into the everlasting fire prepared for the devil and his angels:

All the lost will be there, although not to enjoy the pleasures of sin with one another as many would like to believe. Rather, they will suffer in the presence of one another's agonies and torments. All the lost will be there including the most evil, disgusting and vile people who have ever lived.

Satan and his angels and demons will also be suffering in torments there.

6. **It is eternal.**

> **Matthew 25:46** (NKJV) [46] And these will go away into everlasting punishment, but the righteous into eternal life."

Those who teach that the lost are either annihilated or ultimately reconciled to God after a time of reformatory suffering are in gross error. This fact is seen in those many passages which teach the everlasting nature of the conscious punishment of the lost.

> **Daniel 12:2** (NKJV) [2] And many of those who sleep in the dust of the earth shall awake, Some to everlasting life, Some to shame *and* everlasting contempt.

> **Matthew 18:8** (NKJV) [8] "If your hand or foot causes you to sin, cut it off and cast *it* from you. It is better for you to enter into life lame or maimed, rather than having two hands or two feet, to be cast into the everlasting fire.

> **2 Thessalonians 1:9** (NKJV) [9] These shall be punished with everlasting destruction from the presence of the Lord and from the glory of His power,

> **Revelation 20:10** (NKJV) [10] The devil, who deceived them, was cast into the lake of fire and brimstone where the beast and the false prophet *are.* And they will be tormented day and night forever and ever.

> Cf. 2 Peter 2:17; Jude 7, 13; Revelation 14:11

This then, was the place of eternal torment for all men but for the grace of God. The eternal rewards and blessings of the redeemed are inconceivable and inexpressible (Isaiah 64:4), and the eternal punishments of the lost are too!

THE NATURE OF THE ETERNAL REWARD OF THE RIGHTEOUS

Just as God originally created the heavens and the earth, so He will create new heavens and a new earth, untainted by sin or its effects:

> **Isaiah 65:17** (NKJV) [17] "For behold, I create new heavens and a new earth; And the former shall not be remembered or come to mind.

> **2 Peter 3:13** (NKJV) [13] Nevertheless we, according to His promise, look for new heavens and a new earth in which righteousness dwells.

> **Revelation 21:1** (NKJV) [1] Now I saw a new heaven and a new earth, for the first heaven and the first earth had passed away. Also there was no more sea.

God will also create a "New Jerusalem" where He will reign forever:

> **Revelation 21:2** (NKJV) [2] Then I, John, saw the holy city, New Jerusalem, coming down out of heaven from God, prepared as a bride adorned for her husband.

The following are some of the characteristics of the life of the redeemed in this eternal state:

1. We will have unrestricted, personal fellowship with Jesus Christ.

> **John 14:3** (NKJV) [3] And if I go and prepare a place for you, I will come again and receive you to Myself; that where I am, *there* you may be also.

This will be the greatest thing we will experience for eternity. Gates of pearl, streets of gold and walls of jasper are all wonderful, but they will pale in comparison to the beauty of His face.

> **Revelation 21:3** (NKJV) [3] And I heard a loud voice from heaven saying, "Behold, the tabernacle of God *is* with men, and He will dwell with them, and they shall be His people. God Himself will be with them *and be* their God.

> **Revelation 22:4** (NKJV) [4] They shall see His face, and His name *shall be* on their foreheads.

2. **There will be no dead religion there.**

> **Revelation 21:22** (NKJV) [22] But I saw no temple in it, for the Lord God Almighty and the Lamb are its temple.

There will be no boring ceremonies or rituals – just the joyful, eternal reality of fellowship with God!

3. **Those who overcome will reign with Jesus for eternity.**

> **Revelation 22:5** (NKJV) [5] There shall be no night there: They need no lamp nor light of the sun, for the Lord God gives them light. And they shall reign forever and ever.

> **2 Timothy 2:12** (NKJV) [12] If we endure, We shall also reign with *Him.* If we deny *Him,* He also will deny us.

> **Revelation 3:21** (NKJV) [21] To him who overcomes I will grant to sit with Me on My throne, as I also overcame and sat down with My Father on His throne.

4. **We will inherit all things.**

> **Revelation 21:5** (NKJV) [5] Then He who sat on the throne said, "Behold, I make all things new." And He said to me, "Write, for these words are true and faithful."

5. Everything will be new. The old sin-tainted world will be gone forever (Rev. 21:5).

6. There will be no more sea.

> **Revelation 21:1** (NKJV) [1] Now I saw a new heaven and a new earth, for the first heaven and the first earth had passed away. Also there was no more sea.

In this life, the seas set the boundaries of the nations, but in the eternal state, there will be no more division or separation between people.

7. There will be no more death, sorrow, crying or pain.

> **Revelation 21:4** (NKJV) [4] And God will wipe away every tear from their eyes; there shall be no more death, nor sorrow, nor crying. There shall be no more pain, for the former things have passed away."

Death and suffering are the wages of sin. At the cross, sin was judged eternally, and there will be no more sin or its effects for eternity for the redeemed.   For ever and ever there will be no suffering or pain whatsoever!

> **Revelation 22:3** (NKJV) [3] And there shall be no more curse, but the throne of God and of the Lamb shall be in it, and His servants shall serve Him.

The final removal of the curse of sin is spoken of by the prophet Isaiah:

> **Isaiah 25:7-8** (NKJV) [7] And He will destroy on this mountain The surface of the covering cast over all people, And the veil that is spread over all nations. [8] He will swallow up death forever, And the Lord GOD will wipe away tears from all faces; The rebuke of His people He will take away from all the earth; For the LORD has spoken.

The curse of sin, in all its forms, will be gone forever!

8. **There will be no darkness.**

Revelation 21:25 (NKJV) [25] Its gates shall not be shut at all by day (there shall be no night there).

Revelation 22:5 (NKJV) [5] There shall be no night there: They need no lamp nor light of the sun, for the Lord God gives them light. And they shall reign forever and ever.

Revelation 21:23 (NKJV) [23] The city had no need of the sun or of the moon to shine in it, for the glory of God illuminated it. The Lamb *is* its light.

God, Himself, will be the Light of the righteous for eternity.

9. **There will be no sin or temptation.**

Revelation 21:27 (NKJV) [27] But there shall by no means enter it anything that defiles, or causes an abomination or a lie, but only those who are written in the Lamb's Book of Life.

Only those with righteous natures will be there. There will be no devil or demons there. Eternity will be without sin or temptation of any kind.

2 Peter 3:13 (NKJV) [13] Nevertheless we, according to His promise, look for new heavens and a new earth in which righteousness dwells.

10. **In the New Testament, a number of "crowns" are described as being part of the believer's reward:**

    a. The Crown of Life (James 1:12; Revelation 2:10; 3:11).

    b. The Crown of Glory (1 Peter 5:4).

    c. The Crown of Rejoicing (Philippians 4:1; 1 Thessalonians 2:19).

    d. The Crown of Righteousness (2 Timothy 4:8).

e.   The Incorruptible Crown (1 Corinthians 9:25).

11. We experience full knowledge.

1 Corinthians 3:12 (NKJV) [12] Now if anyone builds on this foundation *with* gold, silver, precious stones, wood, hay, straw,

This does not mean we will know everything. Only God is omniscient, and we shall learn from Him forever. However, there is much that is a mystery to us now that we shall understand clearly then.

12. We will enjoy His glory.

John 17:24 (NKJV) [24] "Father, I desire that they also whom You gave Me may be with Me where I am, that they may behold My glory which You have given Me; for You loved Me before the foundation of the world.

While all believers will be saved, just as there are degrees of suffering among the lost, there will be degrees of glory among the righteous. In 1 Corinthians 15, Paul says that there will be a difference between the glorified bodies of the redeemed. They will all be the same kind of glorified body, but there will be different orders of glory among them.

1 Corinthians 15:41-42 (NKJV) [41] There is one glory of the sun, another glory of the moon, and another glory of the stars; for *one* star differs from *another* star in glory. [42] So also *is* the resurrection of the dead. *The body* is sown in corruption, it is raised in incorruption.

13. We will serve the Lord forever.

Revelation 22:3 (NKJV) [3] And there shall be no more curse, but the throne of God and of the Lamb shall be in it, and His servants shall serve Him.

What a privilege it will be to serve God unhindered with a full revelation of His will, growing in the knowledge of Him forever!

14. We will experience perfect rest.

> **Revelation 14:13** (NKJV) [13] Then I heard a voice from heaven saying to me, "Write: 'Blessed *are* the dead who die in the Lord from now on.' " "Yes," says the Spirit, "that they may rest from their labors, and their works follow them."
>
> Cf. Isaiah 11:10; Ezekiel 34:14-15; Hebrews 4:1

This does not mean we will be inactive in heaven because we have seen that eternity will be filled with joyful, fulfilling service to the Lord. However, we will have rest from all the trials, labors and strivings of this life.

15. We will experience total satisfaction.

Every care will be forgotten, and every need will be supplied. Perfect bliss forever! Jesus truly will be "all we need."

Some have questioned how we could possibly enjoy total satisfaction in the eternal state when there will be different rewards for the righteous. Will we be tempted to be jealous of someone who receives a greater eternal reward than us? The answer is certainly, "No." For one thing, there will be neither sin nor temptation to sin in eternity. Furthermore, each of us will be entirely satisfied with the reward and degree of glory that we possess. Imagine two glasses of water. Each is a different size although both are full. One glass has more water than the other, but both are full as they can be. That is what it will be like in eternity. There will be different degrees of reward and glory between the righteous, but each one of us will be "full" and entirely, eternally satisfied.

16. We will experience unspeakable joy.

ᶦ **EXCURSUS: INFANT BAPTISM**

It is surely an important matter that across Christendom infant baptism (*paedobaptism*) is widely practiced. This is true for Eastern Orthodoxy, Roman Catholicism, and many Protestant denominations. Consideration of this, I believe, belongs to an excursus: a digression from the New Testament pattern of believers' baptism. Some of the arguments for infant baptism will be given with response following.

Household baptisms

The household baptisms in Acts in all likelihood included infants and children who were also baptized. Since Lydia "and her household" were baptized, this probably included children not yet of believing age. With the household as an organic unit, Lydia's faith would make valid the baptism of all members. The Philippian jailer was told by Paul, "Believe in the Lord Jesus Christ, and you will be saved, you and your household," thus declaring that on the basis of the jailer's faith both he and his family would be saved. Hence, although household baptisms do not necessarily prove infant baptism, such baptism seems likely on the basis of family solidarity.

We may first respond by observing that "household" in the New Testament does not necessarily include infants and small children. For example, in John 4, the servants of a Capernaum official brought word to him that his son was healed by Jesus; as a result "he himself believed, and all his household" (v. 53). "His household" probably included the servants and members of the official's family without reference to children. This is even clearer in the story of the Roman centurion Cornelius, who "feared God with all his household" (Acts 10:2). When Peter arrived to preach the gospel, Cornelius "had called together his kinsmen and close friends" (v. 24). It was they – household, kinsmen, and friends – who later believed and were baptized (vv. 43-48). There is no suggestion that his faith and baptism encompassed children too young to believe.

Now looking particularly at the instance of the Philippian jailer, it is a serious misreading of the Scripture to say that his faith would suffice for his household. If we had only the words, "Believe in the Lord Jesus, and you will be saved, you and your household," that might be claimed. However, immediately following this injunction is this statement: "And they [Paul and Silas] spoke the word of the Lord to him and to all that were in his house" (Acts 16:32). Clearly "all … in his house" were people of age capable of hearing and believing the word of God: thus likely his wife and older children. Shortly after that "he and all his household" (v. 33 NASB). Finally, "he … rejoiced greatly, having believed in God with his whole household" (v. 34 NASB). In no sense whatever is this an account of one person's faith including others – a supposed solidarity. Rather, all in his household heard and believed and were baptized in connection with their own personal faith. Infants obviously were not included.

Lydia's household may or may not have included her own family. She was a business woman, a seller of purple goods, residing in Philippi; but she had come from the distant Asia Minor city of Thyatira. Her household (no mention is made of a husband) may then have included various business helpers, perhaps servants. Thus the baptism of Lydia and her household may not refer to family or children at all. If it does, the same thing may apply as with the Philippian jailer: they would have been of age to hear and believe and thus be baptized along with Lydia.

Another significant household baptism (not previously mentioned) is that of Stephanas, Paul writes, "I did baptize also the household of Stephanas" (1 Cor. 1:16). It might be possible to visualize infant baptism in this statement except for the fact that Paul later says, "Now, brethren, you know that the household of Stephanas were the first converts in Achaia, and they have devoted themselves to the service of the saints" (1 Cor. 16:15). This household sounds rather adult!

All in all, the household evidence for infant baptism is very weak. Its advocates usually admit that it is presumptive evidence (there is no direct statement anywhere that children were baptized); however, even to say that much is questionable. Incidentally, in one account that does not mention households, the wording, as we have noted, simply is this: "They were baptized, both men and women" (Acts 8:12). Are we to presume that children are included in "men and women"? The question hardly merits a serious answer. There is no adequate evidence – even presumptive – for infant baptism in any way of the household narratives.

Circumcision and baptism

Since infant boys received circumcision under the old covenant, so should infant children under the new covenant. For both circumcision and baptism are signs and seals of God's covenant of grace that includes not only adults, but also their children. Baptism, which of course is still more inclusive – females as well as males – is nonetheless a parallel to Old Testament circumcision. Both practices demonstrate that a covenanting God includes the whole family. Thus infant circumcision leads properly to infant baptism. The overarching concept is that of the one covenant of grace (Old Testament and New) to which children of

Christian believers now belong; therefore, they should receive the sign and seal of baptism.

By way of response it is important, first, to recognize that there is a connection between circumcision and baptism. Paul refers to both circumcision and baptism in Colossians 2:11-12: "In him you were also circumcised, in the putting off of the sinful nature, not with a circumcision done by the hands of men but with the circumcision done by Christ, having been buried with him in baptism and raised with him through your faith in the power of God" (NIV). Paul, however, is obviously not talking about physical circumcision "done by ... men," which does include infants, but about spiritual circumcision "done by Christ," which includes only those who believe in Him – that is, those who are "buried with him in baptism." Thus the parallel is between spiritual circumcision and spiritual baptism, both of which relate only to active believers in Jesus Christ. Accordingly, there is no way that this passage can be properly used to link infant circumcision and infant baptism.

Again, in reflecting on Old Testament circumcision of infants it is important to note that such was done purely on the basis of physical descent. Abraham, to be sure, received circumcision as a sign and seal of his own faith. Recall Paul's statement about this: "He [Abraham] received the sign of circumcision, a seal of the righteousness that he had by faith while he was still uncircumcised" (Rom. 4:11 NIV). However, not only Abraham was circumcised, for God had commanded, "Every male among you shall be circumcised ... it shall be a sign of the covenant between me and you. He that is eight days old ... every male throughout your generations" (Gen. 17:10-12). Thus, regardless of the faith (or lack of it) among parents, the sign of the covenant must be made. Thus, again there is a great difference between the sign and seal of circumcision based on physical birth and that of baptism, which relates to spiritual rebirth. Because circumcision was given to infant boys in the old dispensation is therefore utterly no reason for giving baptism to infant children in the new covenant.

The basic error lies in the failure to recognize the *difference* between the old and new covenants. Doubtless there is a similarity, for it is the same covenanting God who graciously acts for His people. However, it is a great mistake to say, as many adherents of infant baptism do, that because God included the natural descendants of Abraham, adults and children alike, in the old covenant, He includes the children of believers in the new covenant. Rather, in the new covenant *in Christ,* only those are included who come to personal faith in Him, and in that faith they are baptized.

Jesus' blessing of children

Jesus declared, "Let the children come to me, do not hinder them; for to such belongs the kingdom of God. Truly, I say to you, whoever does not receive the kingdom of God like a child shall not enter it" (Mark 10:14-15). Then the text adds, "And he took them in his arms and blessed them, laying his hands upon them" (v. 16). The words of Jesus, plus His open reception of children, have caused some to imply the validity of infant baptism. But all of this is special pleading. First, the main emphasis in the passage is not on Jesus' reception of children, but on the childlike attitude of trust and openness that one must have to receive the kingdom of God. Not to children, but "to such", belongs the kingdom. Second, Jesus assuredly does bless the children, but blessing has no real connection with baptism. We may recall that Jesus' only recorded reference to water baptism was that it was to be given to "disciples" – "baptizing them" (Matthew 28:19). Thus, those who come to Christ in active faith, not those who are brought to Him, as were the children, are to be baptized. The attempt to relate Jesus' blessing of children to infant baptism is quite misguided.

Actually, the proper use of the texts regarding Jesus' blessing children and taking them in His arms is not for infant baptism, but for infant dedication. It is altogether fitting that parents should bring forward their infants and small children for dedication to the Lord and that the pastor would take the children in his arms for a blessing. It is also altogether fitting that at some later time, when the child has arrived at a responsible decision of faith, he or she come forward and receive baptism. As a matter of fact, infant baptism as practiced in most churches is actually more of a dedication service than a baptism. All that is needed is to omit the water, take the infant up in the arms, and bless as Jesus did! Some years later, it will be the privilege and responsibility of one who was dedicated as an infant to come forward on his own and receive Christian baptism.

It is indeed important for infants and little children to be brought to Christ for His blessing, but it is urgent that the church not confuse baptism with dedication. Baptism belongs to the day – and only that day – when a person makes public confession of his faith in the Lord.

God's prevenient grace

The baptism of an infant magnifies God's prevenient grace in that the child is incapable of responding to God's action in this sacrament. The infant is unknowing and helpless, so in baptism he is totally the recipient of God's grace. Such baptism accordingly attests that long before a person is capable of decision, God has already acted on his behalf.

God's prevenient grace is a precious truth, namely, that God's grace is always primary (for example, in regeneration and sanctification), but grace calls for personal response. Infant baptism unfortunately denies this, because it affords no place for the response of repentance and faith.

The seed of faith and vicarious faith

In infant baptism, faith is operative either as a tiny seed planted in the child's heart or as a vicarious faith on the part of those who bring the child to baptism. From the former perspective it is affirmed that normally the seed will grow until the day when the child can make his own confession. From the latter, it is held that the surrounding faith (of parents, godparents, and congregation) serves vicariously for the faith of the child so that he is truly renewed in baptism.

Neither the seed of faith, nor vicarious faith, is adequate to the New Testament understanding of baptism. "He who believes and is baptized will be saved" (Mark 16:16). Only those who actively believe are to be baptized; thus saving faith is more than a seed and cannot be accomplished vicariously. Moreover, repentance is required at the time of baptism (recall Acts 2:38); this can hardly be done at the time of infant baptism or by proxy. All in all, personal, conscious, even heartfelt faith is essential.

Original sin

Since all persons born into this world come with the guilt of original sin, there is need for baptism as early as possible to remove this guilt and stain. Otherwise infants who die prematurely will be forever cut off from the presence of God. Infant baptism is essential to remove the inherited guilt of original sin so that babies, if they die, may go to heaven.

Even though it is true that infants are not born in innocence – the human race is sinful in nature – baptism is surely not the way to remove the heritage of sin from infants. It is far better to say that even as Jesus blessed the infant children by taking them into His arms, if they die before an age of accountability, He will apply His saving work to them and receive them into heaven.

Further, it is obvious that this view of the removal of the guilt of original sin in regard to infants again points to the error of baptismal regeneration.

Promise regarding children

The earliest proclamation of the gospel by Peter in Acts about repentance, baptism, and the gift of the Holy Spirit (2:38) continues with these words: "For the promise is to you and to your children and to all that are far off, every one whom the Lord our God calls to him" (39). Since children, against a background that specifies baptism, are included in the promise, they rightly may be baptized.

First, a careful reading of Acts 2:38-39 and the background of these verses will show that in the first place Peter is referring to the gift of the Holy Spirit, not salvation (contained in the words "repent," "be baptized," and "forgiveness of sins"), which is promised to all whom God "calls to him" (thus who have received salvation). Hence it is misguided to view the baptism of anyone as included in the promise. Second, Peter's words about children cannot imply infant baptism, since the whole background of repentance and faith calls for conscious decision, and only in that context can baptism occur with the resulting promise of the gift of the Holy Spirit. Third, "your children" is properly understood as "your sons and your daughters" (v. 17) – not your infants – those of responsible age. In every way, to view Peter's words as undergirding the practice of infant baptism is without warrant.

Early church practice

Since there is sufficient evidence of early church practice of infant baptism, we may safely assume the propriety of its continuation to the present day.

The problem with this statement is that the evidence for infant baptism in the first century is nonexistent and meager, if at all, in the second century. It is only at the beginning of the third century (A.D. 200) that the first clear-cut statement about infant baptism is found, namely, in the writing of Tertullian, in which he opposes what seemed to be a growing tendency toward infant baptism! After Tertullian – and despite his efforts – infant baptism became more and more the prevailing practice throughout Christendom. By the time of Augustine (fifth century), infant baptism was officially sanctioned by the whole church.

It is apparent that the propriety of infant baptism cannot be based on early-church evidence for its practice. Paedobaptists are often determined to find it there – even they likewise search the New Testament for evidence – but it is all to no avail. Candidly, one suspects that the practice of infant baptism so dominates much biblical and historical research that it is a matter of seeking justification rather than truth. Since the church at large (Roman Catholic, Eastern Orthodox, Protestant) practices infant baptism, this fact for some is basically all that is needed: surely the church could not be wrong in so important a matter. Church tradition, no matter how wide-spread, *must* never become the norm of Christian truth and practice.

We have viewed the arguments for and against infant baptism. It is not my intention to exaggerate this matter, since baptism whenever it is done is not as fundamental as that to which it points, namely, salvation. However, infant baptism, if nothing else, does cloud the issue, and in many ways it affects both the church's witness and the practical experience of its members. Hence, my concern is to call those churches that practice infant baptism to seriously reconsider what they are doing and make every effort to reinstate the baptism of believers.

www.ingramcontent.com/pod-product-compliance
Lightning Source LLC
Chambersburg PA
CBHW071418090426
42737CB00011B/1504